The European Convention and the Future of
European Environmental Law

Europa Law Publishing, Groningen 2003

K. Ramakrishn

The European Convention and the Future of European Environmental Law

Prof. Jan H. Jans (Editor)

The Avosetta Series (1)

Proceedings of the Avosetta Group of European Environmental Lawyers

Europa Law Publishing is a publishing company
specializing in European Union Law.
For further information please contact Europa Law
Publishing via email: info@europalawpublishing.com
or visit our website at: www.europalawpublishing.com.

Typeset in Scala and Scala Sans, Graphic design by
G2K Designers, Groningen/Amsterdam

NUR 828; ISBN 90-76871-13-2

British Library Cataloguing-in-Publication Data
A catalogue record for this book is available from the
British Library

Preface

The *Avosetta Group* is a small informal group of lawyers whose main purpose is to further the development of environmental law in the European Union and its Member States. *Avosetta* is the Latin name of a rare bird which resulted in the European Court of Justice establishing far-reaching principles of European nature protection law in the *German Leybucht Case*. The group held its inaugural meeting at Bremen University in January 2001. It has its own website on www.avosetta.org.

Those participating in *Avosetta* are invited due to the recognition of their distinction in European environmental law, and they take part in a personal and independent capacity. Nevertheless, *Avosetta* discussions aim to reflect a comprehensive cross-section of legal cultures within Europe, and will generally include up to two participants from each Member and accession States.

This book contains the papers submitted at the *Avosetta* meeting on October 11 and 12, 2002, held in Amsterdam called: *The European Convention and the Future of European Environmental Law*. Furthermore, the book contains the resolution adopted at the Amsterdam meeting.

J.H. Jans
Amsterdam, February 2003

Table of Contents

CHAPTER 3 **Division of Competence between Member States and the EC**
Prof. Dr. Astrid Epiney

CHAPTER 4 **EU Environmental Policy and the Civil Society**
Prof. Dr. Jan H. Jans

CHAPTER 5   **The EC's External Competence and the Protection of the Environment**
Dr. Massimiliano Montini

CHAPTER 6   **The Future Role of the ECJ in the Development of European Environmental Law**
Dr. Ludwig Krämer

CHAPTER 7   **Enlargement and its Consequences for EU Environmental Law**
Prof. Dr. Gyula Bándi

CHAPTER I

Environmental Principles in Community Law

Gerd Winter*

1 Overview of the Community principles

The EC Treaty in the field of environmental policy distinguishes between goals, principles and objectives to be taken into account in preparing Community environmental policy. The objectives contained in Article 174 (1) EC enable, via Article 175 (1) EC, the Community's competences to decide what action is to be taken. Because they at the same time give the exercise of Community competences a substantive orientation they must be seen as principles.

The principles guide not only environmental policy. Inasmuch as they belong to the core tasks of the Community and/or count among the essential goals of the Union as seen respectively in Article 2 EC ('a high level of protection and improvement of the quality of the environment') and in Article 2 EU ('sustainable development') they must be accorded a higher value as compared to other principles not mentioned as a core task.

The integration principle in Article 6 EC (also found, with slight variations, in Article 37 of the Charter of Fundamental Rights of the European Union) plays a special role, because it cannot stand in isolation. Rather, it transposes the principles of environmental policy of Article 174 EC into the other policies of the Community and qualifies this diagonal effect (as will be clarified) by the principle of sustainable development.

Looking at Community law, we can distinguish ten separate environmental principles which themselves express perspectives on environmental law:
- the principle of a high level of protection of the environment;
- the principle of sustaining and improving the quality of the environment;
- the principle of promoting measures at the international level;
- the principle of taking regional factors into consideration;
- the principle of precaution;
- the principle of prevention;
- the principle of rectification at source;
- the polluter pays principle.

The above named principles may seem to be uncompromising. However, Article 174 (3) EC puts them on a more realistic footing. According to Article 174 (3) in preparing its policy Community law shall take account of:
- the available scientific and technical data;
- regional differences in environmental conditions[1];
- advantages and drawbacks;
- economic and social development of the Community, and
- balancing the development of the regions.

---

[*]   Translated by Eric Allen Engle.

[1]   Being already part of the principles this aspect is twice reiterated.

It is noteworthy that sustainability is not directly named as a principle of environmental policy but is seen as both a task of the Community and as a qualification of the principle of integration.

In the following text we will examine the legal effects of environmental principles (paras. 2 to 4) and what conceptual content some of them have (para. 5). As to their legal effect one should distinguish between the governed body, namely: Community organs (para. 2), Member States (para. 3), and enterprises (para. 4). In each case the inquiry is into whether reform proposals for the new European Constitution are to be enacted.

2 Legal significance of the principles vis-à-vis the Community institutions

Whether the principles of environmental protection have legal significance or whether they are only statements of policy goals is contested. There are of course some decisions of the ECJ which undoubtedly impute legal value to the principles (and even the objectives to be taken into account when forming Community environmental policy). The issue, however, has not thereby been resolved because upon closer inspection some core points of controversy appear to have not yet been decided by the ECJ. In order to obtain clarity as to these points it is useful to distinguish between various functional contexts in which the principles have effect.

We can distinguish four such functional circumstances:
- the empowering of decisional competence to the Community;
- the shaping of decisional competence by the Community;
- the imposition of a duty on the Community to act;
- the empowerment of the Community to intervene in the field of guaranteed fundamental rights.

As will be shown next, in order to understand the question of the legal effect of the principles it is recommended to distinguish between instances:
- where the principles make Community action possible – i.e. an *enabling function* as in cases one and four
- where the principles shape or even trigger Community action – i.e. a *directing* function as in cases two and three.

The difference that these functional connections make shall be reconstructed out of the casuistic nature of the Community's case law.

2.1   Enabling functions

2.1.1   Enabling the exercise of Community competences

In the *BSE* case the ECJ drew on the principles of precaution and prevention in order to justify the legal measures taken by the Community which in connection with the BSE crisis were directed against the export of British beef. In the judgement the legal concept of 'acting under uncertainty' enabled Community action:

'Where there is uncertainty as to the existence or extent of risks to human health, the institutions may take protective measures without having to wait until the reality and seriousness of those risks become fully apparent.'[2]

The principle is thus imputed a legal significance in the sense of enabling the Community to act.

On the other hand, secondary legislation can also exceed the margin of legislative discretion which the enabling function of the environmental principles open up. One example of this given by the ECJ is the *Standley* case.[3] Standley, a farmer, brought an action against British laws which were founded upon a Community Directive. That Directive prescribed that the Member States must designate bodies of water with high levels of nitrate and limit intensive animal husbandry in the corresponding zones. On this point the ECJ stated:

'As regards the polluter pays principle, suffice it to state that the Directive does not mean that farmers must take on burdens for the elimination of pollution to which they have not contributed.'[4]

From this one can conclude that the court would have appreciated the act as a violation of the polluter pays principle if the Directive had burdened the person who was not the source. A violation of the principles could consequently overturn a Directive.

---

[2]   Case C-180/96 *United Kingdom* v. *Commission* [1998] ECR I-2265 (para. 99)

[3]   Case C-293/93 *Standley* [1999] ECR I-2603. The relevant passage is in paragraphs 55 and 56 which reads: 'It is true that the action programmes which are provided for in Article 5 of the Directive and are to contain the mandatory measures referred to in Annex (3) impose certain conditions on the spreading of fertiliser and livestock manure, so that those programmes are liable to restrict the exercise by the farmers concerned of the right to property. However, the system laid down in Article 5 reflects requirements relating to the protection of public health, and thus pursues an objective of general interest without the substance of the right to property being impaired.'

[4]   Case C-293/93 *Standley* [1999] ECR I-2603 (paragraph 51)

The enabling function in cases of the exercise of competences by the Community outside the field of environmental policy where environmental protection must be respected by the application of the integration clause (Article 6 EC) is of particular significance. It is for example admissible that the agricultural competences founded on the Directive on pesticides serve the goal not only of protecting plants through the use of pesticides but also to protect the environment from pesticides. On the other hand, if those measures exceed the goal of environmental protection, for example by going beyond the limits of the precautionary principle, they would be illegal and void.

2.1.2 Enabling encroachments on basic rights

Environmental principles can further be drawn upon to justify encroachments on basic rights. This has only rarely occurred however. In comparison to the frequent opposition of basic rights (in particular guarantees of professional freedom and property) and environmental protection in German domestic law, it is astonishing how seldom fundamental rights in the Community have been invoked as a bulwark against Community environmental measures (though this can sometimes be explained by the standing requirements of Article 230 (4) EC).

Standley, however, can be seen as a case which does oppose fundamental rights and Community environmental principles. Standley argued (unsuccessfully) that an EC Directive was an encroachment on his property right. In response the ECJ stated that the exercise of basic property rights could be subjected to limitations in so far as

'*those restrictions in fact correspond to objectives of general interest pursued by the Community and do not constitute a disproportionate and intolerable interference, impairing the very substance of the rights guaranteed*'.[5]

The protection of public health can be such a goal. The Directive serves these ends, as the Court briefly indicated, in a way that follows the principle of proportionality.[6]

Although the ECJ speaks of public rather than human health, it may in fact mean the goal and principle of human health in the sense of Article 174 (1) second indent EC,[7] which the ECJ did not however specifically mention. It could even be drawing on the principle and goal of environmental protection in the sense of Article 174 (1) first indent. For our purposes it is important to remem-

---

[5] Case C-293/93 *Standley* [1999] ECR I-2603 (para. 54).

[6] Case C-293/93 *Standley* [1999] ECR I-2603 (paras. 54, 56).

[7] Krämer (2002b) at 135.

ber that a Community goal like the protection of health can legitimise encroachments on basic rights and thus has a legal significance at least to that extent.

The same holds true for cases in which the ECJ draws on the principle of proportionality as a principle which is independent of fundamental rights. Here, likewise, the court looks for an end which will justify the means and meet the test of proportionality. *Safety High-Tech* is an example that illustrates exactly that search. There the ECJ determined that the prohibition of a certain chemical in connection with the goal of environmental protection was in fact a proportional Community act and thus a permissible exercise of Community power.[8]

2.1.3   Contextualising criteria

Deploying the full scope of environmental principles in the context of the enabling function is in fact possible. Environmental protection (via precaution or prevention) or resource protection against irrational use is possible without questioning the Community competence or conflicting with fundamental rights. However, when the enabling function is at issue the criteria named in Article 174 (3) EC are to be considered. For example, in *Safety High-Tech* the criterion of available scientific and technical data was drawn upon.[9]

In addition, the enabling function opens up arguments *a maiore ad minus*. Those arguments help to identify the core meaning of the principles. For example, arguing *a maiore ad minus*, when action is permissible because of the precautionary principle (in so far as this is sufficient in a given situation), action for the avoidance of dangers is also permissible. When a high level of protection is permissible a lower level of protection is at least permissible.

2.2   Directive functions

Directive functions can be attributed to the principles when they lay down specifications for the exercise by Community organs of a competence norm. This attribution does not relativise but rather encourages action. The obligations that the directive functions of the principles impose are even more marked when, in a situation of otherwise complete passivity or even political resistance, they compel the Community's organs to act.

The Court of Justice has expressed itself on directive functions mostly in the somewhat ironical cases where it was the addressee of a Community measure who complained that the Community measure did not go far enough. The plaintiffs in such cases, whose environmentally injurious acts were enjoined by Community law, appealed that the Community had failed to also (or instead)

---

[8]   Case C-284/95 *Safety High-Tech* [1998] ECR I-4301 (para. 58).

[9]   Case C-284/95 *Safety High-Tech* [1998] ECR I-4301 (para. 48).

punish the other 'sinners'. The argument can be designated as 'the other as well'. The more normal case – where a Community organ, a Member State or a third party who benefits from the Community measure files the complaint – has not yet been decided by the courts.

There are two possible versions of an obligation which may be derived from a principle and shall be treated in turn: firstly, the obligation that the Community legislator must handle complex environmental problems comprehensively and not just incrementally, and, secondly, the obligation that each single problem must be handled to the full extent of the legal standards.

2.2.1 The duty to make use of comprehensive action

Safety High-Tech is particularly relevant as an example thereof. A regulation for the protection of the stratospheric ozone layer prohibited the use of partially halogenated CFCs. The producer, *Safety High-Tech*, argued that CFCs could not be singled out and forbidden without also forbidding halones; for halones which (without controversy) have a higher potential than CFCs for destroying the ozone layer and, in addition, (unlike CFCs), also have a green house effect. Because of the failure to consider the green house potential of halones the general obligation of the protection of the environment was violated; further, because of the failure to consider halones' higher potential to destroy the ozone layer the specific command of a 'high level of protection' was also violated. The ECJ replied, on the basis of ex-Article 130r (now Article 174), that

> '*it does not follow from those provisions that Article 130r(1) of the Treaty requires the Community legislature, whenever it adopts measures to preserve, protect and improve the environment in order to deal with a specific environmental problem, to adopt at the same time measures relating to the environment as a whole.*'[10]

Although this answer is basically reasonable the Court could have gone somewhat further by making use of a German legal construction, namely the *Konzeptgebot* ('planned approach'). The *Konzeptgebot* which was introduced by the *Bundesverwaltungsgericht* may be invoked in situations in which a complex set of problems must urgently be solved but are difficult to handle because of limited instrumental and administrative capacity. Due to this complexity the issues do not have to be solved in one stroke. Rather, the public authorities may proceed step-by-step in singling out individual actors if this is based on a broader plan providing for systematic further action in the future.

In *Safety High-Tech* the application of the *Konzeptgebot* would have meant requesting an overall plan for the phasing out of both CFCs and halones. It

---

[10] Case C-284/95 *Safety High-Tech* [1998] ECR I-2603 (para. 44).

seems that, in fact, there was such a plan in order to fulfil the obligations of the Montreal Protocol. It was defensible to first tackle CFCs, where ready substitutes exist, and then to address the thornier question of halones (which have since indeed been banned).

In *Standley* the *Konzeptgebot* would have required one to ask whether the Directive stood within the framework of a general concept of combating all nitrate sources in order to judge the burdens which arose therefrom on agriculture. Instead the Court of Justice satisfied itself with an isolated consideration of the contribution of farming to nitrates.

2.2.2   The duty to attain a high level of protection

Genuine cases in which a Community measure absolutely and not only in relation to others remains below an attainable level of protection have not yet been explicitly dealt with by the European courts. However, the ECJ in the case of *Standley* does imply the possibility that an environmental protection measure can fail to attain the high level of environmental protection required by Article 174 EC. The ECJ found that this standard had in fact been met as a comparison with the laxer measures of the Montreal Protocol shows. Because the court treated this issue only implicitly the question cannot be considered having been decided.

In conclusion the case law of the European courts comes close to attributing binding value not only to the enabling but also to the directive functions of the environmental principles. However the court's statements are often implicit. We must therefore examine the related doctrinal debate in order to clarify the issue.

2.2.3   Legal doctrine

Considerations of constitutional policy
The EC is not a state but an international organisation for the realisation of certain goals. While states seldom have tasks specifically enumerated in their constitutions, the European treaties in contrast do contain a number of such duties. Considering the nature of the Community there is no reason why the implementation of its duties should not be seen as a question of law. In fact, the duties, in so far as the establishment of the single market was concerned, have always been taken as legally binding as a matter of course. In one case – the duty of a common transport policy according to Article 71 EC – even a complaint for inaction by the Community was filed.[11] Why should environmental policy duties not also figure as legal duties?

---

[11]   Case 13/83 *EP* v. *Council* [1985] ECR 513 (para. 49). It is true, however, that the duty of the Community to act under Article 75 (now Article 71) was more concretely formulated than that of Article 174 EC.

One might object – as the ECJ does in *Safety High-Tech* and *Standley*[12] – that the Member States can always enter into the breach so long as the Community organs do not act. But this is hardly convincing, because the Member States, due to competition or other considerations, often do not strive for a high level of protection. Just as in the field of the establishment of the single market in the field of environmental protection the EC must act as a watchdog defending a public good against the self-interest of the Member States.

Considerations of legal philosophy

One basic argument against the obligatory character of the principles is that if they were binding law then that would strangle the political decision-making process of the Community. However, the principles, even if they are accepted as legally binding having directive power to compel a turgid legislator to act, do possess sufficient flexibility in order to keep political space open. This tension is most appropriately represented in the concept of principles widely accepted by German legal doctrine. According to the German view, particularly influenced by Robert Alexy, principles are defined as being legally binding but open to balancing against other principles.[13] This very character of being open for balancing principles are to be distinguished from rules which have to be applied in any case.

In the Anglo-American literature, as far as it follows Ronald Dworkin, principles are seen as legally binding only to the extent that they contain individual rights. These are to be distinguished from 'policies' which serve not individual but collective goals:

> 'Arguments of principle are arguments intended to establish an individual right; arguments of policy are arguments intended to establish a collective goal. Principles are propositions that describe rights; policies are propositions that describe goals.'[14]

Dworkin apparently has in mind the common law, which, nourished by the legal profession and common sense, balances the spheres of individuals against each other:

> 'The origin of these (i.e. some principles applied in a certain court case) as principles lies not in a particular decision of some legislature or court, but in a sense of appropriateness developed in the profession and the public over time.'[15]

---

[12] Case C-284/95 *Safety High-Tech* [1998] ECR I-4301 (para. 43); Case C-293/93 *Standley* [1999] ECR I-2603 (paras. 46, 48).

[13] Alexy (1986).

[14] Dworkin (1977) at 90.

[15] Dworkin (1977) at 40.

However, the sense of appropriateness to which Dworkin refers can also emerge in relation to issues of collective goals. In fact basic administrative law requirements such as *audiatur et altera pars* and *natural justice* are certainly also to be regarded as principles. Principles can also be codified, either by ordinary legislation or on the constitutional level – the latter being the more appropriate level because of its more general language. Therefore nothing speaks against accepting principles as grounding public interest and by that having binding legal (as opposed to mere political) significance. That is even more true when principles are grounded not only in custom but also in legislation or a constitution.

The legal character of principles may be questioned from yet another perspective, namely the French post-modern view. According to Nicolas de Sadeleer the raging contemporary interest in the principles is the result of the loss of centralised state law making.[16] The principles have a replacement function as they structure new rules – but in a fragmentary and casuistic manner.[17] Thereby, however, their legal character is definitively recognised because it is a matter of building structures of legally binding rules out of or via principles. Even[18] directive functions of the principles on the legislator are recognised which is a somewhat surprising position for a post-modernist because it appeals to the hierarchical relationship of the constitution and the legislator when the constitution enacts such principles. This view has been applied to the environmental principles of the EC Treaty – with very similar results to those sketched here on the basis of a more traditional 'modern' view of how laws are developed.[19]

To see a legal provision as a principle means that if applied in a specific case it can be balanced against other (conflicting) principles.[20] Whilst the hierarchical ordering of principles is problematic in the abstract the law may attribute one principle relatively higher value than another, which means that it at least has a *prima facie* priority which shifts the burden of proof to the defenders of the counter-principle.[21] If there is no predefined *prima facie* priority this must be constructed *ad hoc*. The author suggests a general rule of balancing, proposing that the higher the degree of non-fulfilment or impairment of one principle, the greater must be the importance of the fulfilment of the counter-principle.[22]

---

[16] Cf. De Sadeleer (2002).

[17] De Sadeleer (2002) at 258 *et seq.*

[18] This is the case of de Sadeleer who expressly takes a post-modern view.

[19] Cf. de Sadeleer (2002) at 306 *et seq* and 322 *et seq.*

[20] Alexy (1986) at 88 *et seq.*

[21] Alexy (1986) at 146.

[22] An example of such hierarchisation is in Article 6 (4) of the Habitats Directive: There the protected demands of the rare species and habitats are given priority over interests in their use. However, compelling public interests can overcome this protection. Such interests must again give way to the core demands of nature (namely in the area of prioritised ecological zones) unless the public interest in their use is also a core interest (namely the interests of public health and safety).

In the area of environmental law the judiciary could also develop relative priorities of principles of environmental protection both in relation to other environmental principles and to principles supporting the use of environmental resources.[23] For example, in the case of a conflict between the principle of health and of environmental protection health will have priority with the reservation that environmental protection may have a higher value in certain core areas. Another example is the case of conflict between the free movement of goods and environmental protection – environmental protection has priority according to the case law of the Community.[24]

Considerations of methodology

One of the arguments against the legal (and not programmatic) obligation of the directive function of the principles is simply that their content is very uncertain.[25] However, the courts have often shown that elusive legal language can be filled with content by case-related reasoning.

The ECJ takes a rather cautious stance in this respect. In *Safety High-Tech*, following its usual case law, it stated that:

'*in view of the need to strike a balance between certain of the objectives and principles mentioned in Article 130r and of the complexity of the implementation of those criteria, review by the Court must necessarily be limited to the question whether the Council, by adopting the Regulation, committed a manifest error of appraisal regarding the conditions for the application of Article 130r of the Treaty.*'[26]

Some more guidance than the mere arbitrariness test may be derived from a closer look at the meaning, aim and context of the principles. A core and a penumbra of the principles may be distinguished. When the core of a principle is damaged this leads to the illegality of the measure which is then void. The core could be defined somewhat in the way of *a maiore ad minus*: when measures combating risks may be regarded as a mere programmatic duty, measures to defend against serious dangers should be taken as a legal obligation. When a high level of environmental protection may be regarded as a mere programmatic obligation a minimal level of protection should be taken as binding. When measures, which improve the environment are programmatically obligatory, measures which sustain the environment are to be regarded as legally obligatory.

---

[23] See Kahl (1993) at 166 *et seq.*

[24] See e.g. Case 120/78 *Rewe-Zentral AG* v. *Bundesmonopolverwaltung für Branntwein* [1979] ECR 647.

[25] See Krämer (2002b) at 137.

[26] Case C-284/95 *Safety High Tech* [1998] ECR I-4301 (para. 37).

2.3 Conclusion

We should ask in conclusion whether the above has conse-
quences for the present constitutional debate at the EU. Should the question of
the legal character of the environmental principles be answered by reformulat-
ing Article 174 EC? I believe that the answer is no. The problem is one of legal
construction rather than constitutional decision. The text as it stands provides
sufficient grounds for both a reticent and a more ambitious interpretation. The
solution must be elaborated by the courts and legal scholarship.

3 Legal significance of the principles with regard to the Member States

Up to this point the discussion has only considered the Community as the object of environmental principles. However, Member States can
also be addressed by them. Our reasoning here is again guided by distinguish-
ing between directive and enabling functions.

3.1 Enabling functions

The following justifications for Member States derogating from
or supplementing the Communities' principles of environmental law arise out
of the enabling function of the principles:
- the justification that Member States may encroach on basic freedoms;
- the justification that Member States may go further than EC secondary
  law;
- the justification of a Member State's right to grant subventions and other
  limitations to competition law.

3.1.1 Encroachments on basic freedoms

Since *Danish Bottles* the environmental principle of protection
is recognised as a justification for encroachments by Member States on the basic
freedom of movement of goods.[27] The same is true of the principle of the protection of human health. The *Toolex* case shows this in particular as human health
is affected there not directly through products but indirectly through envi-

---

[27] Case 302/86 *Commission* v. *Denmark* [1988] ECR 4607 (para. 9). For an overview see: Temmink (2000)
at 61-102.

[28] Case C-473/98 *Chemical Inspections* v. *Toolex* [2000] ECR (para. 38). The case concerns the prohibition
of trichlorethylen which also spreads via environmental processes.

ronmental causal chains such as air and water pollution.[28] In the *Bluhme* case the protection of biodiversity as a legally protected interest was recognised.[29] In *PreussenElektra* the climate was similarly recognised.[30] With respect to the principles of Article 174 (2) EC there is case law on the rectification-at-source principle (*Ursprungsprinzip*). This served in *Walloon Waste* as an admissible justification for Belgian import restrictions on waste.[31] However, in other cases the opportunity for corresponding recourse was missed. For example, in *Dusseldorp*, which addressed Dutch export restrictions on waste intended for recycling[32], the ECJ could have relied on the effectiveness of recycling in domestic or foreign installations as a criterion for allowing or disallowing export restrictions; this criterion could have been derived from the principle of the rational use of resources provided by Article 174 (1) third indent EC.[33]

The legal construction of how environmental concerns are related to Article 28 EC is not yet entirely clear.[34] Earlier case law had regarded environmental protection as a unique category of legal justification besides Article 30 EC but limited its application to measures which did not distinguish between domestic and foreign products.[35] In *Bluhme* and *PreussenElektra*, at the latest, the ECJ had projected that separate category into Article 30 EC itself. This had the effect that measures which treat domestic and foreign goods differently – which was the case in *PreussenElektra*, in which foreign electricity producers was not granted the privilege granted to domestic producers of regenerative energy to sell their excess capacity back to the local power grid at a guaranteed price – could be thereby justified. In terms of legal construction the result was reached by a broad understanding of the clause 'the protection of health and life of humans, animals or plants' contained in Article 30 EC.

As a result the notion of 'life of humans, animals or plants' in Article 30 is somewhat overstretched. For instance, in the *Bluhme* case the protection of a species of bee against displacement by other species of bee was given as an example of the protection of animal life.[36] Similarly in *PreussenElektra* the policy of climate protection and the use of renewable energy sources was designated as a policy which serves the goal of protection of life and health of humans, animals and plants.[37]

---

[29] Case C-67/97 *Ditlev Bluhme* [1998] ECR I-8033 (para. 33)

[30] Case C-379 *PreussenElektra* [2001] ECR I-2099 (para. 73).

[31] Case C-2/90 *Commission v. Belgium* [1992] ECR I-4431 (para. 34).

[32] Case C-203/96 *Dusseldorp* [1998] ECR I-4075.

[33] The Dutch government did not raise the issue of recycling effectiveness. As a consequence the court was not compelled to invoke that criterion. See Winter (2000) at 657 *et seq.*

[34] See Jans & von der Heide (2003) at 287 *et seq.*

[35] See Case 302/86 *Commission v. Denmark* [1988] ECR 4607.

[36] Case C-67/97 *Ditlev Bluhme* [1998] ECR I-8033 (paras. 33, 38).

[37] Case C-379 *PreussenElektra* [2001] ECR 2099 (para. 75).

In view of this mismatch of wording and meaning it would be desirable if, in the course of reforming of the EU constitution, Article 30 EC were reformulated to include the environment as a whole. This could be done by inserting the words 'and of the environment' after 'the protection of health and life of humans'.

In connection with this, one further problem of the interpretation of Article 30 EC may be addressed, namely the question of cross-border paternalism of a Member State in relation to the protection of environmental goods situated elsewhere. It is still not entirely clear how far the Member States' restrictions on the single market can be justified by the protection of environmental goods in other Member States, in third states, or in areas outside of any sovereign jurisdiction.

Two questions must thereby be distinguished: first is the question whether the concept of 'animals and plants' in Article 30 EC (and/or 'environment' as suggested above) encompasses only animals and plants within the territory of a Member State. This is clearly to be denied, because the text refers to animals and plants without mentioning borders thus reflecting the fact that ecosystems do not coincide with political borders. Second, one can ask whether other legal texts or principles limit the competence to act. To this belong, first, possible secondary law, which was the case in *Gourmetterie Van den Burg*, in which the ECJ determined that the Red Grouse (a species of bird) was, according to Directive 79/409, able to be legally hunted in Scotland, and thus that its import could not be prohibited by the Netherlands.[38] Other limitations follow the territorial principle of international law, which, however, does not completely preclude regulations with application abroad, but permit them if a connection to the regulating state exists. Still other limitations are also found in international treaty law, in particular in the GATT and in trade related environmental treaties, which will not however be addressed here.

Asking once more whether anything clarifying the cross-border issue should be put into the new constitution it seems that inserting the term 'environment' into Article 30 EC as a protected good suffices to enable the cross-border application of environmental principles. The restrictions provided by EC secondary law and international law need not be made explicit because they are self-evident.

3.1.2 Justification of going further than secondary law

In the area of secondary law Member States can, according to Article 95 (4) and (5) EC and/or Article 176 EC, under certain circumstances enact regulations which go further than Community law. The particular

---

[38] Case C-169/89 *Gourmetterie van den Burg* [1990] ECR 2143 (para. 15). Krämer convincingly comments that the court should have applied Article 14 of Directive 79/409 which indeed provides the possibility of going further. See Krämer (1993) at 157 *et seq.*

preconditions are of no interest here. The only relevant point for our consideration is the question of the applicability of environmental principles. They come
into play as specifying the direction into which complementary Member State
action can move. Thus Article 95 (4) and (5) EC allow for complementary action
'relating to the protection of the environment'. The same is implicit in Article
176 EC. Thus any complementary action must result in greater environmental
protection. The principles contained in Article 174 (2) EC are drawn into Article
95 (4) and (5) EC by the integration clause and into Article 176 through direct
reference to Article 174. They open up the potential space for, but also mark the
limits of, complementary acts. For example, a Member State making use of Article 95 (4) EC can draw upon the precautionary principle when the Community
secondary legal act is limited to defence against danger.

As all of this is more or less clear and reasonable there is no need for any
change in the treaty text.

3.1.3   Enabling national limitations to competition law

Environmental objectives can justify national measures, even if
they have the effect of limiting market competition and would normally be inadmissible because of Article 87 EC. Although they are not (with the exception
of natural catastrophes) expressly mentioned in the admissible circumstances
listed in Article 87 (2) and (3) EC, they arise within the framework of general
concepts such as, e.g., 'aid to promote the execution of an important project of
common European interest' or 'to facilitate the development of certain economic
activities' (Article 87 (3) paras. b) and c)).[39] Projecting environmental protection into these general concepts must be seen not only as decisions which may
be freely made via politics but are also grounded on the integration principle of
Article 6 EC.

With respect to the importance of environmental protection and the fact that
the valid exceptional bases have a distinct bias towards economic development
it is submitted that 'environmental protection' should be inserted as an independent ground for an exception to the principle of the prohibition of subsidies
which hinder market integration.

Member States can distort cross-border competition not only by subsidies but
also by public undertakings as well as by legislation which encourages cartels
or provides monopoly rights. That is of course in principle forbidden, with
respect to cartels through case law[40] and with respect to exclusive monopoly
rights and public undertakings via Article 86 (1) EC. Environmental protection

---

[39] For examples from the casuistic nature of the Commission in granting exceptions see Jans & von der
Heide (2003) at 352 *et seq.*

[40] Jans & von der Heide (2003) at 335 *et seq.*

can in these cases have the effect of justifying such otherwise impermissible goals.[41] This leads to the question whether this should be explicitly stated – as e.g. in Article 81 (3) and 86 (2). However, as cartels and public undertakings are not a central instrumentality for environmental protection, it is submitted that environmental protection need not be explicitly mentioned in either Article 81 or Article 86. The anyway applicable integration clause in Article 6 EC is strong enough to project that principle into the working area of the competition principle.

3.2   Directive functions

Directive functions of the environmental principles vis-à-vis the Member States are less apparent than enabling functions. Certainly the Member States are not bound in so far as their own area of competence is concerned. However in so far as they apply Community secondary legislation and thereby have a certain margin of appreciation they are also under a duty to pay proper heed to the environmental law principles of the Community.[42] This would be a consequential application of the case law in *Wachauf* (which is also codified in Article 53 of the Charter of Fundamental Rights of the European Union), namely that the Member States when applying Community law are bound by the fundamental rights and principles of the Community.[43] That the integration principle of Article 6 EC is nowhere anchored in the national constitution of any Member State is of particular interest in this regard. This could lead to the consequence that the Member States when applying Community law outside the realm of environmental law (say for example energy law) would have to respect the environmental principles of Article 174 EC, including, for example, the principle of the rational use of natural resources.[44]

In terms of doctrinal construction the difficulty persists that both Article 6 and Article 174 in their plain meaning are not directed at the organs of the Community, while the fundamental rights, because of their jurisprudential character, have more room for interpretation and completion. For this reason a clause is recommended for the new European constitution which would oblige the Member States to respect the environmental principles in their application of Community law. Thereby disequilibrium could at the same time be abolished because the Member States are obligated to observe the basic freedoms of the

---

[41]   For examples see Jans & von der Heide (2003) at 335 *et seq.* and 338 *et seq.*

[42]   See Jans & von der Heide (2003) at 23.

[43]   Case 5/88 *Hubert Wachauf v. Bundesrepublik Deutschland* [1989] ECR 2609 (para. 19).

[44]   Similar suggestions have been made by: Macrory (2001) at 8; De Sadeleer (2000) at 112, with further examples.

Community whilst environmental protection limiting basic freedoms is only a power of the Member States but not an obligation.[45]

4 Legal significance with regard to enterprises

The environmental principles of the EC Treaty have direct legal effect even for the actions of enterprises. There the enabling function stands at the forefront: enterprises are in principle prohibited from acts which hinder competition. However, anti-competitive acts may be permissible if they are geared to serve the goal of environmental protection.

The possibility to anchor the environmental principles in the European constitution as duties of enterprises or as general duties of the citizen is as yet undiscovered. This thought may appear very far-reaching, but the radix of this thought is relativised when one recalls that there are rights with direct effect on individuals, in particular the fundamental rights and basic freedoms. Then why not obligations as well? The question however requires greater examination in particular with regard to how far the Member States recognize constitutional duties and their experiences with them.[46]

The environmental principles have an enabling function with respect to certain agreements between undertakings which limits cross-border competition. These are, according to Article 81 (2) EC, in principle void. They can, however, when they serve environmental goals, be valid or admissible. This also holds similarly true for the case of market dominance according to Article 82 EC. For example, if an enterprise demands that its supplier maintains certain environmental standards the anticompetitive effect could be permitted. The particularities shall not be dealt with here. We simply note that the environmental principles are not specifically mentioned in Articles 81 and 82 but are projected into these provisions by way of the integration principle of Article 6 EC. In order to augment their weight it ought to be considered whether environmental goals should be specifically refered to in Article 81 (3) EC.

A similar question is posed for enterprises with exclusive economic rights or with tasks of general economic interest (Article 86 (2) EC). For example, an exclusive economic right for the recycling of waste by a given enterprise can

---

[45] The Avosetta Group has suggested the following formulation: 'Subject to imperative reasons of overriding public interests, significantly impairing the environment or human health shall be prohibited.' To be found at: www.avosetta.org. Because the proposition not only binds the Member States but also binds the Community and does not refer to the principles in Article 174, it would be simpler to add a paragraph to Article 174 which says that Article 174 (1) to (3) must also be respected by the Member States in so far as they apply Community law.

[46] For the constitutional duties of the citizen under German law see Winter (1997) at 67 et seq.

be justified on environmental grounds.[47] Again, the particularities shall not be treated here. However the question is posed whether environmental grounds should be mentioned next to the 'general economic interest' in Article 86 (2) EC.

5 Semantics of precaution and sustainability

Much has already been written about the conceptual content of the principles. I will thus limit myself to selected questions which concern the most important principles and invite inquiry as to whether the treaties should be accordingly reformed.

5.1 Precautionary principle

The precautionary principle has wandered from German domestic law into Community law. As with most migrants it has been marked thereby and does not have exactly the same meaning as this principle has in German national law. The precautionary principle in European law has both a methodological and a strategic significance. This has been clearly indicated both in the statements of the Commission regarding the application of the precautionary principle[48] and in the new leading case of *Pfizer*.[49] Methodologically the principle provides indicators for risk assessment. Strategically, it provides requirements for the decision whether to intervene. In both cases it incites one to be cautious: in risk assessment, scientific uncertainty is no justification to sound the all-clear but must further be scrutinised as to whether there are at least risk indicators, possibilities of interpolation from known facts, etc. Similarly, as to the decision whether to act, scientific uncertainty shall not be sufficient grounds to abstain from precautionary measures.

In sum, this was stated in *Pfizer:*[50]

'Rather, it follows from the Community Courts' interpretation of the precautionary principle that a preventive measure may be taken only if the risk, although the reality and extent thereof have not been 'fully' demonstrated by conclusive scientific evidence, appears nevertheless to be adequately backed up by the scientific data available at the time when the measure was taken.'

---

[47] See Jans & von der Heide (2003) at 338 *et seq.*

[48] Communication on the precautionary principle, COM (2000) 1.

[49] Court of First Instance, Judgment of 11.9.2002, Case T-13/99 *Pfizer v. Commission.*

[50] Court of First Instance *Pfizer v. Commission*, para. 144.

The principle of precaution in German national law has in addition a substantive and an instrumental dimension. A substantive dimension, in that distant consequences both in time and place, damages to particularly sensitive goods, mere irritations and low probability of damage must be looked into when assessing risk. The instrumental dimension refers to the arsenal of pertinent measures. Precaution means in this context that the best available techniques of damage minimisation must be applied relatively independent of foreseeable damages.[51]

This leads to the question whether this additional significance is represented by the other European principles. If this is not the case then the introduction and possibly codification of additional principles might be considered. In all events, however, the greatest economy must reign in the determination of this issue because the sky of general principles is already quite heavily clouded.

The instrumental dimension is possibly represented in the principle of prevention and the principle of rectification at source (*Ursprungsprinzip*). Prevention is the antithesis of reparation. For example, a permit system would be preventive when compared to monetary liability for damages.[52] The point connecting them is the chain of causation. The principle of rectification at source forces the remedial measures as far forward as possible to the start of the causal chain. This structure allows the measure of the best available techniques to be determined without difficulty: it fixes the measure to the emission process which is the first stage in the causal chain and precedes its diffusion and the effects of the dangerous substance.

Understanding the principles of prevention and of rectification at source as requiring best available techniques seems to be hindered by a comment of the ECJ in *Safety High-Tech*, to which the European Court refers in the *Pfizer* case:

'*Article 130r (2) of the Treaty requires Community policy in environmental matters to aim for a high level of protection. Such a level of protection, to be compatible with that provision, does not necessarily have to be the highest that is technically possible*'.[53]

However, it would be wrong to take this statement as excluding policies oriented at the technically possible. Best technologies are simply not required by the principle of a high level of protection. It follows that best technologies can well be required by other principles such as prevention and rectification at source.

The substantive dimension is hardly present in the principles of Article 174 EC. The problem of damages for particularly sensitive goods, inconvenience and

---

[51] As an example see § 5 I No. 2 Bundesimmissionsschutzgesetz.

[52] Naturally liability for damages also has a preventive effect.

[53] *Pfizer*, para. 49.

low probability of damage to environmental goods leaves us to presume that the corresponding interpretative development will occur in the precautionary principle. In the case of temporal and spatial remote effects genuine principles are emerging giving these effects more weight than the prevention principle would, i.e. the principle of protection of future generations, and a possible principle of protection of the global environment.

Both these principles merit particular attention. I suggest that it should be considered to explicitly add them to the list contained in Article 174 (2) EC.[54] It is submitted that this should indeed be done with regard to the protection of the global environment because it is the mechanics of the global biosphere (the climate, the bio-geo-physical equilibrium, the global water cycle, etc.) which will most probably be the most pressing concern for the coming decades. As for the protection of future generations this concern is already represented by the emerging principle of sustainability.

5.2   Sustainability

Sustainable development is defined as a principle of the EU in the preamble to the EU, as a goal of the EU in Article 2 EU and as a task of the EC in Article 2 EC. One can perhaps describe sustainable development as a directive idea or ideal. Thus its legal signification is not that of a legal principle in the sense proposed here.[55] However, in Article 6 sustainable development is an element of the integration principle. Thus though not itself an independent principle but rather a directive goal, sustainable development does have a legal and not merely political significance via Article 6. Further, sustainable development as a binding legal principle may also be anchored in Article 174 or its equivalent in the new constitution. In any case, given the already existing mention in Article 6 EC, the task is incumbent to give the ideal a more specific meaning which makes it more suited to become a legal principle.

The principle of sustainability, like the precautionary principle in Community law, originally came from German law where it had a long and independent history as a principle of forestry law. In this tradition it is closely associated with the use of natural resources and in particular of those which are renewable.

By this origin the sustainability principle differed from the principle of environmental protection in two regards, one concerning the range of application and the other the conceptual content. With regard to the range of application sustainability did not apply to the utilisation of the environment as a sink for waste. This concern was governed by the principles of avoiding dangers

---

[54] With regard to the protection of future generations see also the proposition by the Avosetta Group *supra* note 45.

[55] See Verschuuren (2003).

[56] Rehbinder (2000) at 721 *et seq.*

to environmental goods and later precaution.[56] With regard to the conceptual content the principle of sustainability is more dynamic than danger prevention and precaution because it does permit the destruction of environmental goods if such destruction were also compatible with the long-term renewability of resources – say, by reforestation. The principles of avoidance of danger and precaution instead sought to identify the exact static boundaries between technical processes and 'the environment' and to determine state of the art as well as tolerance limits.

With the report of the Global Commission for the Environment (the Brundtland Commission) in 1987 a bridge between the 'sink' and 'resource' viewpoints was constructed. The resource view was extended to the environment as a whole, including its utilisation as a sink (i.e. the exploitation of its absorption and degradation capacity). Resource use would be allowed provided that use was consistent with long-term conservation of the environment as a system.[57] Three rules have emerged and have also attained consensus:

1 Renewable resources may only be used to the extent that they may be renewed;
2 Non-renewable resources may only be used to the extent that functionally equivalent substitutes among the renewable resources can be found or developed;
3 Harmful emissions cannot exceed the capacity of the ecosystems to break them down.[58]

A further conceptual dimension which the Brundtland Commission accentuates is the link between economy and ecology. The link between ecology and economy as expressed in the principle of sustainability can be understood in at least two ways. The first understanding views the principle of sustainability as mandating the long-term rational use of environmental goods, i.e. economic activity may use resources but must not exhaust them. From this view of sustainability the point of departure is the environment. The legality of economic activity is thus considered in terms of the limits which the sustained resource has on it. A second understanding stands the first on its head: The principle of sustainability can also be understood in terms of whether an economic activity can be maintained in the long-term without destroying its own natural fundament. Then the point of departure is the economy which in turn conditions the environmental considerations.

---

[57] Cf. Ch. 2 No. 14 of the report: 'So-called free goods such as air and water are also resources.'

[58] Rat von Sachverständigen für Umweltfragen, Umweltgutachten 2002. *Eine neue Vorreiterrolle*, (Stuttgart 2002), Nr. 29.

The proposal of the Brundtland Commission takes the second view. The report speaks in terms of sustainable development, not of sustained resources. Thereby the Commission essentially holds that the concerns of natural resources must be developed within the inner structure and mindset of the economy and technological development.

In the intervening period the interpretation of sustainable development has been further developed as having three pillars: Sustainable development thus stands not only for the sustainable protection of the environment's resources but also for the long-term maintenance and development of economic and social welfare.[59] This extension empties the concept, however, to the point that it becomes unrecognisable and one can easily speak of a simple roll-back of ecological protection.[60] Thus it should be rejected. This rejection must, however, not necessarily return to the old principle of sustained natural resources.[61] The consideration of the ecological economy remains tense and its drama is played out above all as pressure to change the habits and practices of businesses and consumers. In contrast to the three pillar model the principle of sustainable development of the economy sets the economy under the pressure of creativity and innovation.[62] Each pillar does not have its own margin of appreciation; rather they compel the economic and social sphere to fundamental change. One can perhaps speak of sustainable development in an emphatic sense. With that understanding it is commendable that the treaties speak of sustainable development and not of sustainable use of natural resources.

In terms of the new European constitution the result in any event is that Article 6 EC should be adhered to. 'Sustainable development' should, because of its linking function, remain to stand at the beginning of the treaty and not in Article 174 or the corresponding chapter on environmental policy.

It should be considered, however, whether in Article 174 the principle of sustainability of the use of natural resources should be adopted. In that event as has been suggested above, mentioning the protection of future generations could be foregone. Moreover, the clause 'prudent and rational utilisation of natural resources;' in Article 174 (1) EC could be integrated into the new principle.

Conceptualising the principle of sustainable development as part of the integration clause has the doctrinal advantage that environmental protection does not have to be inscribed into the individual competences of politics which primarily aim at other goals but have environmental implications. Neverthe-

---

[59] See the Enquête Commission 'Schutz des Menschen und der Umwelt' of the 13th German Bundestages, *Konzept Nachhaltigkeit – Vom Leitbild zur Umsetzung*, (Bonn 1998).

[60] See Rat von Sachverständigen für Umweltfragen, Umweltgutachten 2002. *Eine neue Vorreiterrolle*, (Stuttgart 2002), No. 31.

[61] See Rehbinder (2000) at 730 *et seq.*

[62] See Rehbinder (2000) at 743.

less, explicitly mentioning the protection of the environment is recommended in those political fields which have a particularly important implication for the environment. This is the case of the common agricultural policy, the transport policy, and the energy policy. Correspondingly in Article 33 (1) EC protection of the environment and sustainable agricultural development should be mentioned as a concern or even elevated to a direct goal of agricultural policy; in Article 70 the protection of the environment and sustainable use of energy resources should be named; and in Article 154 (2) EC a paragraph should be added expressing that the Community has also to take account of environmental protection and sustainable use of energy resources.

6 Conclusions

As far as legal interpretation of the environmental principles is concerned we conclude that they are legally binding not only in so far as they enable possible actions for the Community's organs, Member States and enterprises but also in that they create duties to act which must be fulfilled by Community organs and the Member States.

In terms of legal policy for the new Constitution of the European Union the results are:

- the existing formulations of the principles are in general sufficiently ambitious and have worked adequately. In no case should they be driven back beneath the level of protection which has already been reached. This is particularly true of Article 6 and Article 174 EC.

Furthermore, the following are recommended in order to clarify and complement certain points:

- in Article 30 EC the words 'animals and plants' should be replaced by the words 'environmental protection';
- in Article 33 (1) EC a sub-paragraph f) should be added entitled 'to protect the environment and foster sustainable agriculture';
- in Article 70 EC a second paragraph (2) should be added: 'Thereby the requirements of environmental protection and sustainable use of energy resources are to be observed';
- in Article 87 (3) EC after letter d) an exception should be added: 'Subsidies to encourage the protection of the environment';
- in Article 154 (2) EC a third paragraph (3) should be added which should state 'Further, it takes into account the necessity of environmental protection and sustainable use of energy resources';
- in Article 174 (1) EC the third indent should state: 'according to the sustainable use of resources;'. In paragraph 2 a third sentence should be added

with the following content: 'It serves to protect the global biosphere.' to which another paragraph (5) should be added with the following content: 'Paragraphs 1 to 3 also hold true for the Member States in so far as they apply Community law.'

CHAPTER 2

The Right to a Clean Environment in the Constitution of the European Union

A contribution to the discussion on the integration of the Charter of Fundamental Rights of the European Union into a Constitution of the European Union

Florian Ermacora

1 Introduction

The Convention on the Future of the European Union is contemplating *inter alia* the creation of a Constitution for the European Union. As the guarantee of human rights and fundamental freedoms is considered to be an indispensable element of constitutions of democracies, a working group (working group II Charter/ECHR) has been set up within the framework of the said Convention to discuss both the incorporation of the Charter of Fundamental Rights of the European Union (the Charter), proclaimed by the European Parliament, the Council and the Commission in 2000[1], into an EU Constitution and the accession of the EU to the Convention for the Protection of Human Rights and Fundamental Freedoms (the Convention).

The present discussions on the adoption of a Constitution of the European Union, including a legally binding Charter of human rights and fundamental freedoms, provide sufficient reason to (again) reflect upon a (fundamental) right to a clean environment. So far, neither the Charter nor the Convention contain an explicit right to a clean environment.

Article 37 of the Charter stipulates that a high level of environmental protection and the improvement of the quality of the environment must be integrated into the policies of the Union and ensured in accordance with the principle of sustainable development. While this Article recognizes the importance of environmental protection as part of EC policies, it obviously does not constitute a right to a clean environment.

The present contribution describes the origins of such a right to a clean environment in EU law and outlines the possible shape of such a right. Such a description appears to be useful as the formulation of a (constitutional) right to a clean environment needs to consider existing approaches to such a fundamental right in Community law. To this end it will be analysed whether and, if so, to what extent Community law provides a right to a clean environment or certain elements of such a right. Subsequent to this analysis some advantages of establishing an explicit right to a clean environment in the EU Constitution are discussed. An attempt to formulate a right to a clean environment, including explanatory notes, will conclude the present contribution.

---

[1]   OJ 2000, C 364/01.

2 The right to a clean environment in EC legislation

2.1 Introduction

A right to a clean environment consists of two elements: First, a provision needs to lay down the substance of the granted right for the individual.[2] This substantive right would, however, be of limited value only, if the 'privileged' individual had no possibility to invoke this right before a court or national administration. Consequently, the substantive right needs to be complemented by a *locus standi* given to the privileged individual.[3]

2.2 The right to a clean environment in EC primary legislation

2.2.1 Introduction

Article 6 para. 1 EU Treaty stipulates that the European Union is founded upon the principles of liberty, democracy, respect for human rights and fundamental freedoms, and the rule of law, principles which are common to the Member States. Furthermore, the Union shall respect fundamental rights, as guaranteed by the European Convention for the Protection of Human Rights and Fundamental Freedoms signed in Rome on 4 November 1950 and as they result from the constitutional traditions which are common to the Member States, as general principles of Community law (Article 6 para. 1). These provisions of the Treaty on European Union manifest the respect for human rights and fundamental freedoms at the EU level and try to bridge the gap resulting from the absence of a binding[4] catalogue of fundamental rights in EU law. Accordingly the case law of the European Court of Justice has established a legal system protecting fundamental rights, which is based on the general principles

---

[2] Parts of the legal literature contend that a right to a clean environment consists of three facets: the right of individuals to obtain environmental information, the right to participate in environmental decision making and access to justice in environmental matters (compare the references in Szczekalla (2003) 327, para. 48, note 206). As regards the substantive right, the present contribution is confined to rights providing for the actual protection of the environment, leaving aside, with a few exceptions, the right to obtain environmental information and the right to participate in environmental decision making.

[3] In this sense the German and Austrian legal literature defines as a 'subjective right' as a right which establishes a legal claim (see Ermacora (1988) 5, with further references).

[4] The Charter of fundamental rights of the European Union is as such not binding on the Member States. Compare for all De Witte (2001) 81 *et seq.*

of law as applied in the Member States and as derived from the Convention for the Protection of Human Rights and Fundamental Freedoms (the Convention).[5]

Consequently, the general principles of law as applied in the Member States and as derived from the Convention need to be assessed in order to establish whether or not a right to a clean environment already forms part of EC law. As detailed research into the existence of a right to a clean environment in national constitutions or the case law of the national constitutional courts would be beyond the scope of the present analysis[6], what follows is confined to an assessment of the Convention and the case law of the European Court of Human Rights.

2.2.2   The substantive right to a clean environment in EC primary legislation[7]

The Convention does not contain an explicit right to a clean environment. In various cases the ECHR has had, however, to assess whether and to what extent environmental pollution might violate traditional human rights or fundamental freedoms enshrined in the Convention.

In the case of *López Ostra* v. *Spain*[8] a family in the Spanish town of *Lorca* suffered from gas fumes, noxious odours and similar nuisances emanating from a plant, located at a distance of only twelve metres (!) from the family home. The Court established that the nuisances in question did not seriously endanger the health of the complainants, thus Article 3 of the Convention ('No one shall be subjected to torture or to inhuman or degrading treatment or punishment') had not been violated. Conversely, the Court found that 'naturally, severe environmental pollution may affect individuals' well-being and prevent them from enjoying their homes in such a way as to affect their private and family life adversely'. The Spanish authorities did not take measures which were necessary to cease the plant's operation and were thus responsible for a violation

---

[5] Case 4/73 *Nold* [1974] ECR 491. Along these lines Article 52 para. 3 of the Charter stipulates that in so far as the Charter contains rights which correspond to the rights guaranteed by the Convention, the meaning and scope of those rights shall be the same as those laid down by the Convention.

[6] Most European constitutions expressly recognise a right to a clean environment in one form or another (Article 66 of the Portuguese Constitution, Article 45 of the Spanish Constitution, Article 24.1 of the Greek Constitution, Article 21 of the Dutch Constitution, Article 23 of the Belgian Constitution, Articles 2 and 73-80 of the Swiss Constitution, Article 20a of the German Constitution, Article 14A of the Finnish Constitution, Article 110B of the Norwegian Constitution). Even in those cases where the respective Constitution does not expressly recognise this right, it might be stipulated in framework laws (for example Article L-110-2 of the French Environmental Code).

[7] See also Kley-Struller (1995) 507 *et seq.*; Desgagné (1995) 263 *et seq.*

[8] Judgment 41/1993/436/515 of 9 December 1994.

of the right of everyone 'to respect for his private and family life, his home and his correspondence' (Article 8).

In the case of *Guerra and others* v. *Italy*[9] the ECHR found a violation of Article 8 of the Convention with regard to the residents of houses located at approximately one kilometre from a plant releasing inflammable gas. The Court stated that the direct effect of the toxic emissions on the applicants' right to respect for their private and family life meant that Article 8 was indeed applicable. Both the applicants and the Commission on Human Rights argued that Italy had not only infringed Article 8 but also Article 10 of the Convention, according to which 'everyone has the right to freedom of expression. This right shall include freedom ... to receive ... information...'. In their view this Article had to be construed as conferring an actual right to receive information, in particular from the relevant authorities, on members of local population who had been or might be affected by an industrial or other activity representing a threat to the environment.[10] The Court did not follow this argumentation however.

In the case of *Önerydildiz* v. *Turkey*[11] the ECHR found that the Turkish authorities had violated Article 2 of the Convention ('Right to Life') by not informing persons living close to a non controlled landfill site about the risk of methane explosions which might occur – and had actually occurred – at the landfill site in question.

Against this background and considering recent case law regarding noise disturbances by aircraft[12] it could be stated that according to the determined case law of the ECHR the right to a healthy environment is included in the concept of the right to respect for private and family life.

2.2.3 The procedural right to a clean environment in EC primary legislation

The substantive right to a clean environment provided by the Convention as described in the precedent implies – according to the Convention – the possibility of enforcement within the Member States of the Council of Europe. Consequently, also within EU Member States the possibility to enforce these rights is not preconditioned by a provision in EU law explicitly granting a *locus standi* to individuals in relation to these human rights and fundamental freedoms.

Access to justice explicitly granted by EC primary law is still extremely restricted. Article 230 para. 4 EC limits access to justice to those who are directly and individually concerned. The criterion of individual concern has so far been

---

9   Judgment 116/1996/735/932 of 19 February 1998.

10   Note 52 of the judgment in case 116/1996/735/932.

11   Judgment 48939/99 of 18 June 2002.

understood by the ECJ in such a restrictive way[13] that the actual existence of a right for an individual has played a minor role regarding the access qualification.[14] This situation would have changed fundamentally if the ECJ had followed the line of the Court of First Instance as expressed in the *Jégo-Queré* case[15], according to which the criterion of individual concern would be much easier fulfilled than under the so called *Plaumann* formula. In *Jégo-Queré* the Court of First Instance ruled that:

> *'a natural or legal person is to be regarded as individually concerned by a Community measure of general application that concerns him directly if the measure in question affects his legal position, in a manner which is both definite and immediate, by restricting his rights or by imposing obligations on him. The number and position of other persons who are likewise affected by the measure, or who may be so, are of no relevance in that regard'.*

In *Unión de Pequeños Agricultores*, however, the ECJ dashed all hopes of a wider interpretation of Article 230 para. 4 EC by reiterating the applicability of the *Plaumann* formula.[16]

2.3   The right to a clean environment in EC secondary legislation

2.3.1   The substantive right to a clean environment in EC secondary legislation

(a) Introduction

A general and explicit right of individuals to a clean environment has so far not been incorporated into EC secondary legislation. Certain provisions of EC secondary environmental legislation provide, however, explicit rights on the part of individuals to at least certain aspects of a clean environment. Other provisions of EC environmental legislation are construed by the ECJ as providing such rights for individuals.

---

[12]   Judgment 36022/97 of 2 October 2001 (*Hatton and others* v. *the United Kingdom*).

[13]   Case 52/62 *Plaumann* [1963] ECR 95.

[14]   Also in the 'environmental' case of C-321/95 P *Stichting Greenpeace* ECR [1998] I-1651, the lacking individual concern of the complainants led the ECJ to dismiss the appeal by private individuals against the order of the Court of First Instance (T-585/93 ECR [1995] II-2205) declaring that their application against a Commission decision to grant financial support for the construction of energy generation plants in Spain was inadmissible.

[15]   Court of First Instance, T-177/01 *Jégo-Queré* [2002] ECR II-2365, para. 51.

[16]   Case C-50/00 P *Unión Pequeños Agricultores* [2002] ECR I-6677, para. 37 *et seq.*

(b) Explicit stipulation of rights of individuals

The most obvious example of an individual right within EC environmental legislation to – at least one aspect of a clean environment – is the right to environmental information as set out in Directive 90/313 on the freedom of access to information on the environment.[17] Similarly explicit is the right of the public, provided by Article 6 para. 2 of Directive 85/337 on the assessment of the effects of certain public and private projects on the environment[18] (EIA Directive), to receive any request for development consent and any information on the project gathered under Article 5 of the said Directive. Compare also the forthcoming Directive on Waste Electrical and Electronic Equipment, which will grant individual holders of electrical or electronic waste from private households the right to return such waste free of charge.[19]

(c) ECJ case law on the rights of individuals to a clean environment

The ECJ has discussed the rights of individuals set out in EC environmental legislation on the one hand in the context of the obligation of Member States to transpose Directives into national law, and on the other, in the context of the direct effect of Directives.

Case law on the necessity to transpose the obligations under EC environmental Directives into national law

In case 131/88 the ECJ stated that Directive 80/68 on the protection of groundwater against pollution caused by certain dangerous substances[20] seeks to protect the Community's groundwater in an effective manner by laying down specific and detailed provisions requiring the Member States to adopt a series of prohibitions, authorization schemes and monitoring procedures in order to prevent or limit discharges of certain substances. The purpose of these provisions of the Directive was – according to the ECJ – to create rights and obligations for individuals. The Court found that the fact that a practice is consistent with the protection afforded under a Directive does not justify a failure to implement that Directive in the national legal order by means of provisions which are

---

[17] OJ 1990, L 158/56.

[18] Directive 85/337 as amended by Directive 97/11, OJ 1997, L 73/5. See also Advocate-General *Elmer,* opinion in Case C-72/95 *Kraaijeveld* [1996] ECR I-5431, para. 70, on the individual right set out in this Article.

[19] Article 7 para. 1 of the Proposal for a Directive on Waste Electrical and Electronic Equipment (COM2000/347 final), OJ 2000, C 365 E/184. Cf. Vedder (2002).

[20] OJ 1980, L 20/43.

capable of creating a situation which is sufficiently precise, clear and open to permit individuals to be aware of and to enforce their rights. The assumption of the Court that Directive 80/68 confers enforceable rights on individuals is surprising as none of the stipulations of the said Directive mention individuals, let alone explicitly granting them an individual right to clean groundwater. It could be concluded from this judgment that explicit references to the legal position of individuals in general EC rules, which lay down emission limits or quality standards for water, air or soil, do not constitute a condition for the existence of an individual right.

In a subsequent case[21] the Court explained why implementing national acts need to be binding, thereby granting individuals an enforceable right: Article 2 of Directive 80/779/EEC on air quality limit values and guide values for sulphur dioxide and suspended particulates[22] was imposed 'in order to protect human health in particular'. Thus, the Court suggested that whenever the exceeding of the limit values could endanger human health, the persons concerned must be in a position to rely on mandatory rules in order to be able to assert their rights. Although there was an explicit reference to the protection of individuals by the Directive in this case, the general rule deducted from Case 131/88, according to which such references are not a precondition to affirm the existence of rights of individuals in general EC rules, which lay down emission limits or quality standards for water, air or soil, is not put into question by this judgment.

Case law on the direct effect of EC law

Primarily in earlier cases, but also partly in more recent cases, dealing with the direct effect of provisions set out in EC Directives, the ECJ considered the existence of rights of individuals or at least of favourable legal positions in Directives as a precondition for their direct effect in national law. Consequently, the ECJ analysed the measures concerned as to whether they provide rights of individuals.

Touching upon the core of the present contribution, in the so called *Cava* case[23] the *Tribunale Adminstrativo Regionale* of Lombardy submitted the following question to the ECJ:

'*Does Community environmental law, in particular Article 4 of Council Directive 75/422/EEC of 15 July 1975 on waste, grant to individuals "subjective rights" ('diritti soggettivi') which the national court is required to protect?'.*

---

[21] Cf. Case 361/88 *Commission v. Germany* [1991] ECR 2567, para. 16.

[22] OJ 1980, L 229/30.

[23] Case C-236/92 *Cava* [1994] ECR I-483, para. 8.

While the Court abstained from a general answer to this question, it limited its judgment to the provision of Article 4 of Directive 75/442/EEC on waste[24] and thereby provided certain indications as to its understanding of the rights of individuals.

Article 4 of the said Directive provides:

> '*Member States shall take the necessary measures to ensure that waste is disposed of without endangering human health and without harming the environment, and in particular:*
> *- without risk to water, air, soil and plants and animals,*
> *- without causing a nuisance through noise or odours,*
> *- without adversely affecting the countryside or places of special interest'.*

In the grounds for its answer to the Italian question the Court referred to earlier judgments[25] on the direct effect of provisions of Directives and thereby implicitly confirmed the close relationship between such subjective rights and rights which could be invoked before State authorities under the direct effect doctrine. In the present case, however, the Court found that Article 4 only indicates a programme to be followed and sets out the objectives which the Member States must observe in their performance of the more specific obligations imposed upon them by other stipulations within the Directive. The provision in Article 4 did not – according to the Court – lay down any particular requirement restricting the freedom of the Member States regarding the way in which they organize the supervision of the activities referred to therein. It must rather be regarded as defining the framework for the action to be taken by the Member States regarding the treatment of waste and not as requiring, in itself, the adoption of specific measures or a particular method of waste disposal. The Court concluded as to the status of Article 4 'It is therefore neither unconditional nor sufficiently precise and thus is not capable of conferring rights on which individuals may rely against the State.'

In more recent cases the ECJ has abandoned the requirement that provisions of Directives need to provide individual rights in order to exhibit a direct effect within the Member States. The Court thus agreed on the existence of an objective direct effect of Directives.[26] The *Großkrotzenburg*[27] case revolved around the question whether or not Germany had failed to fulfil its obligations derived from the EIA Directive as the project in question had been authorised without applying the provisions of the Directive, although the time-limit for the transposition of the Directive had already expired at the time of initiating the consent proce-

---

[24] OJ 1975, L 194/39.

[25] Such as Case 8/81 *Becker* [1982] ECR 53.

[26] *Streinz* (1999) para. 403.

[27] Case C-431/92 *Commission v. Germany* [1995] ECR I-2189.

dure. The Court stated[28] that the obligation flowing directly from the Directive to assess the environmental impact of the project concerned has to be considered separately from the question whether individuals may rely – against the State – on provisions of an unimplemented directive which are unconditional and sufficiently clear and precise. In *Kraaijeveld*[29] and *Bolzano*[30], both dealing with a failure to implement the EIA Directive, the ECJ justified the right of individuals to invoke the Directive by the useful effect of the respective Directives, which would be weakened if individuals were prevented from relying upon it before their national courts.[31] In neither of the two cases did the ECJ enter into the discussion as to whether the EIA Directive provides rights or favourable legal positions for individuals.

As a consequence, recent (and probably future) ECJ case law on the direct effect of environmental Directives hardly provides indications as to the existence of the rights of individuals to a clean environment, as the direct effect of Directives in national law can no longer be considered to be dependent on the provision of rights of individuals in the concerned Directive. Furthermore, the *Kraaijeveld* case clarified that even if the Court identifies individual rights, which could be derived from environmental Directives, the respective rights do not need to be rights to a clean environment: the underlying interest in initiating the Dutch court procedure was a purely economic one as the concerned Dutch Water plan would have prevented access to certain navigable waterways which would be ruinous to Kraaijeveld's business, whose economic activity was related to waterways.

2.3.2   The procedural right to a clean environment in EC secondary legislation

As summarised above, individuals can rely on those provisions of environmental Directives which – according to the case law of the ECJ – exhibit direct effect in the Member States. For the time being (and leaving aside questions related to the interpretation of national law in conformity with Directives and state liability due to the infringement of provisions of EC Directives) this is the only general basis in Community law which enables individuals to invoke environmental stipulations before national courts.

The forthcoming Proposal for a Directive on Access to Justice in Environmental Matters, implementing the Convention on Access to Information, Public Participation in Decision-Making and Access to Justice in Environmen-

---

[28] Case C-431/92, para. 26.

[29] Case C-72/95 *Kraaijeveld* [1996] ECR I-5403.

[30] Case C-435/97 *Bolzano* [1999] ECR I-5613, para. 71.

[31] Case C-72/95, para. 56, C-435/97, para. 69.

tal Matters (Aarhus Convention) should fundamentally change this situation: According to the chapter 'Legal Standing' of the Commission working document 'Access to Justice in Environmental Matters'[32] further specified members of the public shall be entitled to have access to environmental proceedings. Those members include concerned members of the public, who have a sufficient interest or who maintain that a right has been infringed, and qualified entities, who do not have to maintain any infringement of a sufficient interest or of a right under certain conditions.

3 The formulation of a human right to a clean environment in the EU Constitution

3.1 Reasons for a right to a clean environment

The preceeding section has shown that international law incorporated into EC law via the fundamental principles of the EC Member States and genuine EC environmental legislation contain important facets of a right to a clean environment. While the formulation of such a human right within the framework of an EU Constitution (or the Treaties) would not therefore introduce a fundamentally new concept into Community law, it would exhibit a number of advantages:

First, the formulation of a right to a clean environment would concentrate the – currently rather dispersed – aspects of such a right in one clause. Such a move would enhance the clarity of the concept and provide legal certainty. In any case the formulation of a right to a clean environment would transfer the initiative on this important issue from the courts, which in the case of the ECHR are not even Community institutions, back to the political actors and finally the legislator. This obviously does not exclude the development of this right by case law.

Another positive effect of creating a proper human right to a clean environment as part of an EU Constitution would be the attention paid to the respect of such a right by the individuals. Already today the lacking or flawed implementation of EC environmental law by the Member States is one of the main deficiencies of environmental protection within the EU. Overall this situation will probably deteriorate further with the accession of the ten new Member States, which in many cases do not have the administrative capacity necessary to control the actual implementation of EC environmental law. The lack of implementation

---

[32] Second Working Document Access to Justice in Environmental Matters of 22.07.2002 prepared by Unit A.3 of DG Environment of the EC Commission; (http://www.europa.eu.int/comm/environment/aarhus/index.htm.

control by public authorities could at least be partly outweighed by individuals defending their right to a clean environment.

Finally, enshrining a right to a clean environment in the EU Constitution would give the protection of the environment an equal ranking with rights such as the freedom to conduct a business (Article 16 of the Charter) or the right to property (Article 17 of the Charter), which could be invoked in order to defend economic interests.

3.2   Proposal for the formulation of a right to a clean environment

'Everyone has the right to a clean natural environment. This right is subject to reasons of overriding public interest. It includes the right to participation in decision making, the right to access the courts and the right to information in environmental matters. A high level of environmental protection and the improvement of the quality of the environment must be integrated into the policies of the Union and ensured in accordance with the principle of sustainable development'.

3.3   Explanatory notes

3.3.1   An anthropocentric right

Those aspects of a right to a clean environment which could be found in existing EC law clearly establish the link between a right to a clean environment and the interests of humans: The ECHR takes the human right to respect for private and family life as a point of departure for the development of its case law on a right to a clean environment. Similarly, the ECJ talks about rights granted to individuals by EC environmental legislation. This anthropocentric approach to a right to a clean environment is understandable as only humans could be the subject of (human) rights. Consequently, a right to a clean environment which could be invoked in spite of the absence of some – at least: possible – impairment of the legal sphere of individuals by the act of environmental pollution in question would hardly fit within the traditional system of human rights.

3.3.2   The link between environmental pollution and the impairment of the legal sphere of individuals

Assuming that the right to a clean environment protects humans, it needs to be established how close the link between interference with the environment and the impairment of individual interests needs to be, in order to consider a violation of the individual's right to a clean environment. In the same context the requirements as to prooving an actual impairment of the interests of the individual do need to be considered. While the constitutional legislator needs to be aware of these considerations, it will without any doubt be the task of case law to elaborate the details of the concept.

The ECHR case law on the protection of individuals against environmental pollution shows that such protection could be ensured by means of established fundamental rights in exceptional cases only: According to the Court the link between the environmental pollution and the impairment of the legal sphere of individuals needs to be very close; high standards are applied as regards proof of the (potential) impairment of individuals. In the case of *López Ostra* v. *Spain* the Court obviously required clear indications that emissions from the plant in question did at least endanger the health of people living in the vincinity (at a distance of 12 meters) of the plant. Also in the case of *Guerra and others* v. *Italy* the applicants, who had been affected by the emissions from the plant, lived close – at a distance of approximately one kilometre – to the concerned installation. And in this case the Court explicitly pointed out that the effect of an act of environmental pollution on the fundamental rights of an individual must be direct in order to violate these rights.

Against this background the added value of a genuine right to a clean environment compared to the protection of the environment by means of established human rights would be to loosen the link between interference with the environment and the impairment of the legal sphere of individuals. Thus, not only the direct effects of environmental pollution but also acts of environmental pollution which exhibit their negative effects indirectly, for example over a certain time period, a certain distance, specific side effects, need to be contestable on the basis of a proper right to a clean environment.

This formulation of a right to a clean environment should, however, not dispense with the need for the concerned individual to prove some sort of causal link between the pollution/degradation of the environment and the possible impairment of traditional interests of individuals, such as their health, family life or property.

3.3.3 Application of the basic principles of environmental policy

The formulation of a right to a clean environment, as the basis of legal measures for individuals against acts of environmental pollution, which do not necessarily impair the legal sphere of individuals directly, would be in conformity with the fundamental principles of environmental policy. These principles include that precautionary and preventive action should be taken, environmental damage should as a priority be rectified at source and that the polluter should pay.[33] Obviously these principles could be better implemented

---

[33] Article 174 EC.

if the concerned individual was in a position to claim protection against acts of
environmental pollution, which might also indirectly lead to the impairment of
other fundamental rights, such as the right to life or to respect for private and
family life. The formulation of the environmental right (and the interpretation
of this right) should thus ensure that such a right comes into play before any
direct infringement of the legal sphere of the individual, such as other fundamental rights, takes place.[34]

3.3.4   Rights which complement the right to a clean environment

As the ECHR pointed out in the case of *Guerra and others* v.
Italy essential instruments of environmental policy, such as the right to environmental information, could not be derived from known rights set out in the Convention, such as the freedom of expression (Article 10). Against this background
it is questionable whether the interpretation of a right to a clean environment,
actually protecting environmental media and thus individuals, would be broad
enough to also include individual rights, which could be considered as ancillary
rights to such a protective right. Thus, such ancillary rights should be explicitly mentioned as rights to a clean environment. In this sense a right to a clean
environment needs to comprise the right to participate in decision making, the
right to access the courts and the right to information in environmental matters.
The explicit mentioning of these rights is furthermore in line with the UN/ECE
Convention on Access to Information, Public Participation in Decision-Making
and Access to Justice in Environmental Matters (Aarhus Convention).

3.3.5   Making the right sufficiently precise

If one conclusion could be drawn from the direct effect doctrine of the ECJ, it is the need to formulate the right to a clean environment
in such concrete and precise terms that individuals could invoke it before the
courts. In particular based on the *Cava* case the right to a clean environment
needs to be unconditional and sufficiently precise to be capable of conferring
rights, on which individuals may rely against the State.

---

[34] Along these lines the European Commission on Human Rights argued in the case of *Guerra and others*
v. *Italy* that Article 10 of the Convention (Freedom of expression) should be considered as granting a
right to environmental information which 'had a preventive function with respect to potential violations
of the Convention in the event of serious damage to the environment and Article 10 came into play even
before any direct infringement of other fundamental rights, such as the right to life or to respect for
private and family life, occurred'.

3.3.6 Consideration of other interests

The right to a clean environment is not absolute. Public, including economic, interests might limit the scope of the right to a clean environment. Such interests however, need to be of overriding importance for the public. For other cases, the proposed formulation ensures that – when balancing varying interests – the interest of environmental protection enjoys at least the same importance as economic rights, such as the right to property or the right of free movement of goods.

CHAPTER 3

Division of Competence between Member States and the EC

Astrid Epiney

1 Introduction

The issue concerning the competence to legislate is one of the key issues of the European convention. In this context, the question is raised in general terms (how should the competence be divided? which methods shall be used for this purpose? should the current system be thoroughly modified?).[1] However, the present paper will focus more specifically on the field of environmental policy. This appears to be useful for at least four reasons: firstly, the methods of dividing competence between Member States and the EC/EU differ in the various areas of the treaty, so as to justify limitation to one domain. Secondly, environmental matters have certain distinctive characteristics, above all an interrelational aspect and difficulties in the implementation process.[2] Thirdly, it seems rather unlikely that the convention (and/or the Member States later on) will really find a general method for the delimitation of competence, which means that the characteristics of the different areas will probably – in one way or another – still play a certain role. Finally, it seems useful in any case to start from the existing situation which requires a particular view of each domain of competence.

Thus, the objective of the present paper can be summed as follows: to analyse the current system for the division of competence in Article 174 *et seq.* EC (para. 2), to illustrate these principles by applying them to the special question of environmental organisations' right of access to justice (para. 3) and, in a final stage, to show that the current system of the division of competence seems – in principle – to be well suited to environmental matters, even if some clarifications could be helpful (para. 4).

2 Division of competence in environmental matters: the system of Article 174 seq. EC

Like many provisions which relate to the competence of the EC, Article 175 EC – which is the relevant legal basis in the field of environmental policy – is based on the principle that the achievement of certain aims should be decisive in answering the question of whether or not the EC has the competence to adopt a certain legislative act. Article 175 EC confers – on the EC – the (general) competence to adopt all measures which should assist in realising the objectives enumerated in Article 174 EC. In other words: the range of the

---

[1] Cf. for example von Bogdandy & Bast (2001); Bungenberg (2000); Bieber (2001); Pernice (2000).

[2] Cf. these particularities with further references Jans (2000), 17 *et seq.*, 135 *et seq.*; Epiney (1997), 3 *et seq.*, 105 *et seq.*; Calliess (2002), Rdnr. 28 *et seq.*

[3] Cf. with further references Epiney (1997), 3 *et seq.*

Communities' competence in environmental matters is determined by the goals formulated in Article 174 EC.

The question which is raised by this system is whether the reference to Article 174 EC could in any way imply a real limitation of the EC's competence. This question must be answered in the negative: the catalogue of aims set out in Article 174 EC is very extensive. Thus, the environmental policy of the EC should contribute to preserving and protecting the environment and to improving its quality, to protecting human health, to using natural resources in a rational way and to promoting international activities in this field. The formulation of these objectives is so broad that it is difficult to imagine a Community measure that does not fall within this catalogue. It would therefore seem that the reference to the objectives of Article 174 EC does not really limit the Communities' competence in the field of environmental policy. It can also be added that the notion of environment in Community law is a very wide one, even if it does not comprise all the conditions which are of importance to a person's well-being: it embraces the natural environment, wheter or not it is modified by human activities.[3]

Nevertheless, the question which arises is whether the explicit indication, in Article 174 EC, that EC policy should (only) contribute to realising the targets mentioned in this provision signifies that certain areas of competence should remain in the hands of Member States, thus implying that EC law acknowledges a sort of 'domestic environmental legislation'. This question must definitely be answered in the negative, for at least four reasons:

- firstly, as pointed out above, the extent of the EC's competence in the field of environmental policy is determined by the purpose of the planned measures to realise the objectives mentioned in Article 174 EC. As a consequence, this criterion is the only one that is relevant in order to determine the limits of the Communities' competence.
- secondly, the reference to the realisation of the objectives of Article 174 EC implies that in principle no area of policy can be immediately excluded from the competence of the EC. In fact, a vast range of measures in numerous areas can, in principle, all contribute to the achievement of the aims mentioned in Article 174 EC.
- thirdly, Articles 174 and 175 EC do not contain any criteria which would make it possible to define the 'domestic competence' of Member States in one way or another.
- fourthly, Article 175 (2) EC confirms the opinion held in this paper: this provision mentions policies which, in principle, definitely fall within the competence of the Member States, so that this provision only makes sense if one assumes that the Community's competence cannot be limited to certain areas but, on the contrary, extends to all material domains,

---

[4] Cf. Jans (2000), 11 *et seq.*; Epiney (1997), 84 *et seq.*

provided that the foreseen measure contributes to the realisation of one of the objectives set out in Article 174 EC.

Finally, I would like to call to mind the principle of subsidiarity (Article 5 (2) EC) which establishes the conditions under which an existing competence can be made use of.[4] As I am discussing the very existence of a competence, I will only evoke this principle in general terms.[5]

3 Concerning the EC's competence to introduce provisions relating to access to justice, especially for environmental organisations

The purpose of the following section is to show that on the basis of the current system, as described above[6], the Community has the competence to introduce, in a general manner, an obligation for Member States to implement a right of access to justice in favour of certain persons, especially environmental organisations.

According to the principle that Article 175 EC includes all measures which contribute to the realisation of the objectives mentioned in Article 174 EC, the Community also has the competence to introduce measures tending to improve the implementation of environmental law. In other words, the scope of Articles 174 and 175 EC is not limited to material provisions but also includes procedural instruments which could contribute to a better enforcement of environmental law and, as a result, to a better protection of the aims pursued. It is therefore relatively undisputed that the Community can – in a particular environmental act – include instruments which are aimed at improving implementation, such as provisions guaranteeing access to justice.[7] This point of view is convincing, because the various aspects of implementation – access to justice included – are very often vital in order to ensure the effectiveness of a legislative act. The issue is often also closely related to material aspects. Finally, the principle according to which the implementation of Community law generally falls within the competence of Member States, leaving them free to settle the modalities ('autonomy

---

[5] Cf. para. 3 of this contribution in relation to the special question of introducing a general right for environmental organisations on access to justice.

[6] Para. 2 of this contribution.

[7] Cf. Krämer (1990), at 156 *et seq.*); Jane Holder/Susan Elworthy, Annotation to Case C-237/90, *CMLRev* 1994, 123 at 132 *et seq.*); Kahl (1993), 144 *et seq.*; Wegener (1998), 85 *et seq.*; Ruffert (1996), 320 *et seq.*; Manfred Zuleeg, *VVDStRL* 53, 190 *et seq.* Cf. in general as regards this question (competence of the Community to rule on aspects related to implementation) Hatje (1998), 95 *et seq.*

[8] E.g. Art. 4 Directive 90/313 on access to information on the environment.

concerning the implementation instruments'), is not in conflict with the opinion set out above: Member States are only autonomous inasmuch as they are not bound by Community legislation, so that the mentioned principle cannot alter the Communities' competence. No material area can be immediately excluded from the Communities' competence since the latter is defined – in the field of environmental policy at least – according to the realisation of specific objectives. Many provisions can be found in the environmental legislation of the EC which touch upon questions of implementation, including aspects of access to justice.[8] Another aspect concerns the various provisions in environmental directives which are relative to questions of public participation.[9]

The real question in this context is whether Article 175 EC also allows the EC to legislate on issues of implementation (including access to justice) independently from a concrete legislative act. In other words: can the Community – on the basis of Article 175 EC – adopt a general directive[10] containing the obligation for Member States to introduce certain implementation measures, including, among other things, guaranteeing a defined access to justice? There could be some doubts as to their right to do so, as there would no longer be a link to a specific legislative act. The Community definitely has the competence to adopt such a general directive. Inasmuch as it is undisputed that the Community legislator can introduce this type of provision in each material legislative act, there is no reason to assume that it could not settle such implementation issues in a general act. As a result, a general process of settling issues of implementation does not give rise to any further questions – as far as the competence of the Community is concerned – other than those raised by an individual introduction in each material legislative act. Furthermore, it is allowed, under Article 175 EC, to introduce – in a general way – measures which will improve the implementation of environmental law, since a better implementation of environmental law contributes to the objectives of Article 174 EC. These measures also include the extension of access to justice, which constitutes one of the classical instruments leading to improved implementation.[11]

The obligation of Member States to introduce instruments of implementation, especially in the field of access to justice, can also be founded in Community legislation which is not based on Article 175 EC but on other dispositions of the Treaty. Article 6 EC makes it clear that environmental matters can also be pursued in other policy areas. Therefore, the competence of the Community to introduce implementation measures must also be extended to acts in these areas. In this perspective, Article 175 EC allows the EC to impose obligations on

---

[9] E.g. Art. 6 (II) Directive 85/337 on environmental impact assessment, Art. 15 (I) Directive 96/61.

[10] In any case a directive would probably be more suitable than a regulation.

[11] See also Ruffert (1996), 320 *et seq.*

[12] The opposite view is defended by Führ/Gerbers/Ormond/Roller, *elni Newsletter* 1994, 3 (6, 8 s.).

the Member States to take special implementation measures. This article can therefore be regarded as an independent legal basis for enacting certain acts containing provisions the objective of which is to improve the implementation of environment-related obligations.

These considerations demonstrate that the competence of the EC to introduce a right of access to justice for environmental organisations is limited to matters which concern the implementation of Community legislation. In other words: the EC can only stipulate an obligation for Member States to introduce a right for environmental associations to invoke a violation of EC law or of national law founded on EC law (as transposed directives). Therefore, the national legislator cannot be obliged to introduce general access to justice for environmental organisations allowing them to invoke a violation of a purely national environmental legislation.[12] National environmental legislation is adopted by the national legislator on the basis of a purely national decision; therefore if the Member States can decide on the adoption of material rules, they must also have the competence to decide how they wish to ensure the implementation of the national legislation and whether or not they want to introduce a right of access for certain persons, especially for environmental associations. The competence of Article 175 EC (in relation to Article 174 EC) only refers to Community legislation and its implementation; Article 175 EC does not lay down any kind of general clause obliging Member States to adopt measures which will ensure a more effective implementation of environmental legislation, even a national one. Therefore, the Community's competence to adopt measures related to implementation has a subsidiary character. On the other hand, these principles do not mean that national legislation can never be the object of a Community obligation to introduce a right of access to justice for environmental associations: the right of access to justice can be justified, provided that the national legislation transposes or implements Community law, since in this case the object of the implementation is – at least indirectly – Community legislation.[13]

In principle, the introduction of a right of access to justice for environmental organisations in the sense mentioned above would also satisfy the requirements of the principle of subsidiarity (Article 5 (2) EC)[14]: Since the deficiency in the implementation of Community environmental law is a recurrent phenomenon,

---

[13] The problem is parallel to the question of the conditions under which the fundamental rights of the European legal order are also binding on Member States. For more details on this problem with further references, see Epiney (1995), 125 *et seq.*

[14] For more details on this principle with special reference to environmental policy, see Jans (2000), 11 *et seq*, who reaches the conclusion that 'an examination of Community environmental legislation in the light of the above guidelines would reveal that probably not one environmental directive or regulation would fail to pass the test.' (p. 14).

the aim of such a measure cannot be achieved – in a sufficient manner – on a national level. It is sufficient that the aim of the measure cannot be, *de facto,* efficiently realised on the level of the Member States; a real impossibility is not required. If environmental associations' right to access is introduced, experience in different States[15] has shown that this instrument improves the implementation of environmental legislation in general so that the aim pursued can be better achieved at the Community level.[16]

4 Conclusion: evaluation of the current system and perspectives for the division of competence in the field of environmental policy

The current system according to which the range of the EC's competence in the field of environmental policy is defined in relation to the objectives of environmental policy, themselves defined in a broad manner, should be maintained. This system makes it possible to react to the relevant and important problems in the field of the environment and to take the necessary measures in order to achieve the desired aims. Furthermore, it is a necessary condition in order to enable the Community to take all measures for a coherent environmental policy. This system also takes into account the interdependence which characterises environmental tasks: very often, the lack of measures in one area brings about important consequences for other areas so that an orientation towards the aims of environmental policy seems to be the best solution for defining the Communities' competence. This means that in the area of the environment there should be no division of competence as regards narrowly and completely defined fields (*sachgegenständlich*), but there should be – in the future as well – a clear reference to the aim of environmental policy in relation to a broad notion of environment. Thus, as in numerous other areas within the EC's competence, its competence in the field of the environment is, on the one hand, defined in relation to a (wide) area (the environment), and, on the other, is

---

[15] See the overview by Epiney (1999), at 486; see also in relation to the situation in different Member States Epiney & Sollberger (2001), 29 *et seq.*

[16] If the EC has the competence to impose an obligation on Member States to introduce access to justice for environmental organisations, the form in which such an obligation should be introduced must be decided upon in a second step. This point is not included in the topic of this paper, but for more details on this subject, see Epiney (1999), at 493 *et seq*).

determined by the effectiveness of the measure in realising the aims defined in the Treaty.[17]

Above all, the maintenance of the current system would have the following consequences:

- From the perspective of the EC, there will/should be no limiting list of areas which can be the object of Community legislation.
- From the point of view of the Member States, there will/should not exist a list of 'reserved domains' in which the Community can in no case take legislative measures. If the competence of the EC is defined in relation to the contribution of a measure to the realisation of certain aims, no substantial field can be excluded from the very outset. In other words, the competence of the EC will/should be defined by its contribution to a certain aim and not by its belonging to a specific domain, so that from a material point of view no domain can be *a priori* excluded from EC legislation.
- Community action does not necessarily require a link to another Member State; the aims actually defined in Article 174 can be dealt with even if there is no link to another Member State.
- Community measures relating to implementation fall within the competence of the EC. Over and above the arguments already mentioned above, it must be pointed out that the limits between material measures and measures only relating to implementation are blurred and in any case difficult to define.
- The division of competence itself should not be determined by the principle of subsidiarity. It does not seem possible to precisely define domains which – on the basis of an application of the principle of subsidiarity – should fall within the competence of the EC and others (only) within the competence of the Member States. Such a system would lead to endangering the realisation of the aims of environmental policy in the EU. Furthermore, it does not seem possible to find the 'right' solution as regards the division of competence, on the basis of a scientific analysis of the principle of subsidiarity.

This plea for maintaining the current system does not mean that there is no need at all to reform the division of competence between the EU and the Member States. However, in my opinion – and this affirmation is not limited to

---

[17] In principle, almost all the competences in the Treaty are defined in that way. They make a distinction essentially by referring to a certain domain (environment, transport etc.) or by the lack of such a reference (as Art. 94 s. EC). So, it would be a fundamental change to alter this system in favour of a sort of enumeration of areas ('*sachgegenständlich*') for which the EC should be competent. Cf. in relation to the current discussion von Bogdandy & Bast (2001); Bungenberg (2000); Bieber (2001); Pernice (2000).

the domain of environmental policy – the need for reform is merely a matter of clearer presentation and formulation of the system of division of competence; the substance – in particular the orientation of the EC's competence towards the realisation of certain aims – should not be changed. Above all, the question of the legislative procedure must be raised, especially in the field of environment policy. Therefore there is no reason (apart from the merely 'selfish' interests of certain Member States) for Article 175 (2) EC to reserve the procedure of unanimity for the domains mentioned in this provision and for it not to lay down the codecision procedure.

CHAPTER 4

EU Environmental Policy and the Civil Society

Jan H. Jans

1 Introduction

The decision-making process in the EU finds it *formal* legitimacy, via the European Parliament and the Council, in elected representatives
of the European people. As the European Parliament stated in its Resolution[1] on
the *White Paper on Governance*[2]:

*'Consultation of interested parties [....] can only ever supplement and never
replace the procedures and decisions of legislative bodies which possess democratic
legitimacy; only the Council and Parliament, as colegislators, can take responsible
decisions on the context of legislative procedures [....]'.*

However, there is no contradiction between broad consultation and the concept
of representative democracy. Therefore, in this contribution I will explore how
environmental non-governmental organisations (ENGOs) can make a contribution to fostering a more participatory democracy and *substantive* legitimacy
within the European Union. In this respect I recall in particular Article 34 of
the Preliminary Draft Constitutional Treaty[3] which sets out the principle of
participatory democracy, by which the institutions are to ensure a high level of
openness, permitting citizens' organisations of all kinds to play a full part in the
Union's affairs.

The European Union is founded, as stated in Article 6 EU, on the principles
of liberty, democracy, respect for human rights and fundamental freedoms and
the rule of law. Principles which are common to the Member States. Of course,
the right of individuals to form ENGOs to pursue a common (environmental)
purpose is a fundamental freedom in any democracy. Increasingly ENGOs are
recognised as a significant component of civil society and as providing valuable
support for a more democratic system of government.[4]

The purpose of this contribution is two-fold. First of all, it aims to provide
an overview of the existing legal relationships between EU environmental policy
making and ENGOs. Secondly, it aims to suggest possible ways to improve and
to strengthen this relationship. I will explore the role of ENGOs in the pre-
proposal stage of policy making; their role during the formal decision-making
process and their role after a formal legal act (directive or regulation) has been
enacted.

---

[1] A5-0399/2001.

[2] COM(2001) 428 final. See for a critical appraisal of the White Paper Eriksen (2001).

[3] CONV 369/02 of 28 October 2002.

[4] Cf. Commission Discussion Paper 'The Commission and Non-Governmental Organisations: Building a
Stronger Partnership'; COM (2000) 11 final, at 4.

2 The pre-proposal stage

2.1 General remarks

Consultation mechanisms form part of the activities of all European institutions throughout the whole legislative process, from policy-shaping prior to a Commission proposal to the final adoption of a measure by the legislature and its implementation. There are, according to the EC Treaty, institutionalised advisory bodies established especially to assist the Commission, the Parliament and the Council, namely the Economic and Social Committee and the Committee of the Regions. However, the role of these bodies does not exclude direct contact between the Commission and interest groups.

In fact, wide consultation is one of the Commission's duties according to the Treaties. Protocol No. 7 to the Amsterdam Treaty on the application of the principles of subsidiarity and proportionality states that 'the Commission should [...] consult widely before proposing legislation and, wherever appropriate, publish consultation documents'.

In this respect we should also note that the specific role of non-governmental organisations (NGOs) is closely linked to the fundamental right of citizens to form associations in order to pursue a common purpose, as highlighted in Article 12 of the Charter of Fundamental Rights of the European Union.

On the possible role of NGOs the Commission has expressed its view in a discussion paper entitled *The Commission and Non-Governmental organisations: Building a Stronger Partnership.*[5] The paper signals a variety of problems:
- cooperation with NGOs is organised differently from one policy area to the next;
- internal Commission procedures are complex;
- there is a lack of funding, funding opportunities and information related to this;
- the Commission should provide better information for NGOs and improve communication with them as a means of building a true partnership.

Partly to overcome these problems the Commission has issued a Communication entitled *Towards a reinforced culture of consultation and dialogue* and has established some general principles and minimum standards for the consultation of interested parties by the Commission.[6] In that Communication the following general principles are acknowledged:
- principle of participation;
- principle of openness and accountability;

---

[5] See footnote 4.

[6] COM (2002) 704 final.

- principle of effectiveness;
- principle of coherence.

With regard to minimum standards the Commission mentioned the following:
- Clear content of the consultation process; All communications relating to consultation should be clear and concise, and should include all necessary information to facilitate responses;
- Consultation target groups; When defining the target group(s) in a consultation process, the Commission should ensure that relevant parties have an opportunity to express their opinions;
- Publication; The Commission should ensure adequate awareness-raising publicity and adapt its communication channels to meet the needs of all target audiences. Without excluding other communication tools, open public consultations should be published on the Internet and announced at the 'single access point';
- Time-limits for participation; The Commission should provide sufficient time for planning and responses to invitations and written contributions. The Commission should strive to allow at least 8 weeks for the reception of responses to written public consultations and 20 working days' notice for meetings.
- Acknowledgement and feedback; Receipt of contributions should be acknowledged. Results of open public consultation should be displayed on websites linked to the single access point on the Internet.

2.2   No legal obligation to consult ENGOs

What is the influence of 'civil society' on environmental policy making by the EU institutions? Legally speaking, there is none. Neither the Economic and Social Committee nor the Committee of the Regions – although both have close contacts with NGOs – can or should be regarded as representing the opinion of the public at large in the decision-making process.

Looking at matters from a legal perspective: dialogue and consultation between with NGOs and the Commission have to be seen within the framework of the decision-making procedures in general and for ENGOs within the framework of Article 175 EC in particular. The specific value of these consultations derives notably from the Commission's right of initiative. In other words: dialogue and consultation with ENGOs must be seen in the perspective of enhancing the quality of the Commission's proposals to the Council and the European Parliament.

ENGOs are clearly recognised as 'stakeholders' in developing European environmental policy making. Timely consultation with ENGOs at an early stage of policy-shaping is increasingly part of the Commission's practice of consulting widely, in particular at the stage before formal proposals are submitted to the Council and the European Parliament.[7]

In this respect it should be noted that the EC signed[8], in June 1998, the 'UN/ECE Convention on Access to Information, Public Participation in Decision-Making and Access to Justice in Environmental Matters', the so called *Aarhus Convention*. The Convention invites the Parties to promote public participation during the preparation of executive regulations and generally applicable legally binding normative instruments that may have a significant effect on the environment. Article 8 of the Convention reads:

'Each Party shall strive to promote effective public participation at an appropriate stage, and while options are still open, during the preparation by public authorities of executive regulations and other generally applicable legally binding rules that may have a significant effect on the environment. To this end, the following steps should be taken:

(a) Time-frames sufficient for effective participation should be fixed;

(b) Draft rules should be published or otherwise made publicly available; and

(c) The public should be given the opportunity to comment, directly or through representative consultative bodies.

The result of the public participation shall be taken into account as far as possible.'

The words 'shall strive to promote' make it clear that this provision is somewhat less than 'hard and fast law'. Anyway, by signing the Convention the EC demonstrated its commitment to ensuring adequate consultation of the public in the process of shaping EC environmental policy. However, measures of the EC institutions to implement the international obligation of Article 8 Aarhus Convention have still to be taken.

2.3 Lessons to be learnt from the 'social dialogue'?

One way of enhancing the role of ENGOs would be to introduce into the EC Treaty a procedure which is similar to what is known as the *social dialogue*. According to Article 138 (1) EC the Commission has the task of promoting the consultation of management and labour at Community level and shall take any relevant measure to facilitate their dialogue by ensuring balanced support for the parties. To this end, before submitting proposals in the social

---

[7] See footnote 4, at 7.

[8] But not yet ratified: see the proposal for a Council Decision on the signature by the European Community of the UN/ECE Convention on access to information, public participation and access to justice in environmental matters; COM/98/0344 final.

policy field, the Commission shall consult management and labour on the possible direction of Community action (para. 2 of Article 138 EC). If, after such consultation, the Commission considers Community action to be advisable, it shall consult management and labour on the content of the envisaged proposal (para. 3 of Article 138 EC). But then again, I am not convinced that a similar provision in the environment chapter of the EC Treaty would be a good idea after all. The legal obligation to consult without reservation seems to be rather rigid and not sufficiently flexible to accommodate the need for swift action, when environmental protection requirements so demand. However, the idea behind the *social dialogue* – i.e. to improve the legitimacy of measures by means of consultations with the relevant stakeholders in society – should be followed up in environmental policy making as well. But I do not see the necessity to include into the treaties a rigid legal obligation to do so. Of course there are other means to enhance a 'European' public debate on environmental affairs.

2.4   Green and White Papers

In particular, the Commission, by issuing 'Green and White Papers', can and does stimulate a public debate. Green Papers focus on a particular area of interest for which the Community has not yet produced legislation, for example the Green Paper on integrated product policy.[9] Primarily, a Green Paper is designed to be a consultative document, addressed to interested parties, individuals, companies, and organizations, all of which are then invited to give their input to any possible future legislation. A time-limit is provided, by when the interested parties are required to submit their comments to the Commission. Usually, although not always, a Green Paper will lead to a Communication, which may lead to an actual proposal for legislation.

White Papers are used as vehicles for the development of policy in areas that have not yet come under existing legislation. The major difference between the two papers is that White Papers focus on broader areas that cover more than one industry, such as the White Paper on environmental liability.[10] These are drawn up as a consequence of an analysis of important policy to the Union as a whole. Specific proposals for legislation may follow in the framework of a White Paper.

Furthermore, the Commission could organise and stimulate – in the pre-proposal stage – aspects like public hearings, society-wide discussions. Not on all, but on the important issues. As far as I can see there are no legal impediments in the current Treaties.

---

[9]   COM (2001) 68 final.

[10]   COM (2000) 66.

3 The decision-making process

3.1 Towards a general application of the co-decision procedure

'Amsterdam' has succeeded in making decision making in the context of the Title on the Environment less complex. The standard procedure is now, according to Article 175(1) EC, the *co-decision procedure*, as regulated in Article 251 EC.

Under this procedure the European Parliament is twice consulted on the measure proposed and has the ultimate power to prevent the adoption of a measure. Although co-decision does not automatically lead to more 'environmentally friendly' legislation, the fact that the co-decision procedure is now the standard decision-making procedure must nevertheless be welcomed.

However, the second paragraph of Article 175 EC states that:

'by way of derogation from the decision-making procedure provided for in Article 175 (1), the Council, acting unanimously on a proposal from the Commission and after consulting the European Parliament, the Economic and Social Committee and the Committee of the Regions, shall adopt:
(a) provisions primarily of a fiscal nature;
(b) measures affecting:
  - town and country planning;
  - quantitative management of water resources or affecting, directly or indirectly, the availability of those resources;
  - land use, with the exception of waste management;
(c) measures significantly affecting a Member State's choice between different energy sources and the general structure of its energy supply.'

Indeed, we have come a long way from decision making by unanimity under the 'old' Articles 100 (now Article 94 EC) and 235 (now Article 308 EC) EEC Treaty to majority voting and a strong role for the European Parliament under an explicit environment paragraph in the Treaty.[11] A final step in the emancipation of European Environmental Law is still to be taken. And that is that all European environmental measures should be subject to majority voting according the co-decision procedure.

3.2 Openness and secrecy in the Council

A related issue is the question of secrecy during the decision-making process. In all Member States the legislator debates in public. Public debate therefore has a very important role in providing legitimacy for legisla-

---

[11] See on this development Jans (2000), Chapter I.

tive acts. The following question had been raised: should the Council meet and debate in public? The impetus to a positive answer to this question has been provided by the Praesidium of the European Convention. In Article 36 of the Preliminary Draft Constitutional Treaty[12] a provision on 'Transparency of the Union's legislative debates' is added which should establish the rule that the leg-islative debates of the European Parliament and of the Council in its legislative form shall be public. I would indeed welcome such a provision. Of course this provision would not only be applicable to decision making on environmental protection, but instead it should have a general scope.

3.3   Delegated decision making

Not unimportant in practical terms are the *comitology* proce-dures. Apart from the decision-making procedures referred to in the Treaty, many standards are set – especially technical standards – by means of delegated legislation.[13] The legal basis for *comitology* in the EC Treaty can be found in Arti-cle 202, third indent:

'To ensure that the objectives set out in this Treaty are attained the Council shall, in accordance with the provisions of this Treaty:

[...]

– confer on the Commission, in the acts which the Council adopts, powers for the implementation of the rules which the Council lays down.

The Council may impose certain requirements in respect of the exercise of these powers. The Council may also reserve the right, in specific cases, to exercise directly implementing powers itself. The procedures referred to above must be consonant with principles and rules to be laid down in advance by the Council, acting unanimously on a proposal from the Commission and after obtaining the Opinion of the European Parliament'.

The 'principles and rules' mentioned in the final sentence of this provision have been laid down in what is being called the Second Comitology Decision.[14]

---

[12] CONV 369/02 of 28 October 2002.

[13] OJ 1999 L 184/23.

[14] Decision 1999/468, OJ 1999 L 184/23; see also the Proposal for a Council Decision amending Decision 1999/468/EC laying down the procedures for the exercise of implementing powers conferred on the Commission; COM(2002) 719 final. Cf. on the duty to give reasons if and when the institutions wants to derogate from the criteria in the Second Comitology Decision: ECJ judgment of 21 January 2003, Case C-378/00 *Commission* v. *Council and EP*, not yet reported in the ECR. The judgment concerned the partial annulment of Regulation 1655/2000 on a financial instrument for the environment.

Delegated decision making, in particular concerning technical standard setting, is quite common in European environmental law. One example is the Waste Directive.[15] This directive contains a number of annexes describing categories of waste, disposal operations and operations which may lead to recovery. Amendments to these annexes are made by means of a committee procedure set out in the directive. This requires a representative of the Commission to submit to the committee a draft of the measures to be taken. The committee must then deliver its opinion on the draft within a given time-limit. If the measures envisaged are in accordance with the opinion, the Commission will adopt the measures. If they are not, the Commission must submit a proposal to the Council, which can then act by a qualified majority. However, if the Council has not acted within a period of three months, the proposed measures will be adopted by the Commission. Other directives on the environment also provide for committee procedures, which may or may not be similar.[16]

The judgment in Case C-378/00, already mentioned in this paper, makes it clear that the criteria of the Second Comitology Decision make clear that the institutions are free to derogate from them, provided they give reasons as to why such a derogation is necessary. Therefore, if and when for environmental reasons the EC institutions feel that it is necessary to derogate from the criteria of the Second Comitology Decision, there is no legal impediment to doing so. There is only a legal duty to give reasons as to why this is necessary. In view of this, I do not see any particular reason either to amend the Second Comitology Decision or Article 202 EC itself, just for environmental reasons.

3.4 Access to information

Access to the environmental information of the institutions is first of all dealt with in Article 255 EC. Any citizen of the Union, and any natural or legal person residing or having its registered office in a Member State, shall have a right of access to European Parliament, Council and Commission documents. This right, however, is subject to 'general principles and limits on grounds of public or private interest governing this right of access'. These principles have been laid down by Regulation 1049/2001 of the Council, Commission and EP.[17]

One major problem regarding access to environmental information concerns the practice of the Commission not to make available to interested citizens information regarding the use of infringement-proceedings against the member

---

[15] Directive 75/442, OJ 1975 L 194/47, later amended.

[16] See for instance Directive 94/67 on the incineration of hazardous waste, OJ 1994 L 365/34, Article 16.

[17] OJ 2001, L 145/43.

states.[18] The legal basis for such a refusal can be found in Article 4 (2) second and third indent of Regulation 1049/2001:

'The institutions shall refuse access to a document where disclosure would undermine the protection of:
- [...]
- court proceedings and legal advice,
- the purpose of inspections, investigations and audits,
unless there is an overriding public interest in disclosure.'

The alternative route via the Member States will, in general, not be available to ENGOs either. The reason for this is that Article 5 of Regulation 1049/2001 states the following:

'Where a Member State receives a request for a document in its possession, originating from an institution, unless it is clear that the document shall or shall not be disclosed, the Member State shall consult with the institution concerned in order to take a decision that does not jeopardise the attainment of the objectives of this Regulation.
The Member State may instead refer the request to the institution.'

Although the case law of the CFI prior to the enactment of Regulation 1049/2001 seems to indicate that these restrictions are within the law[19], we have to point to a relevant development in the Aarhus Convention. Article 4 (4) (c) provides that

'a request for environmental information may be refused if the disclosure would adversely affect
[...]
The course of justice, the ability of a person to receive a fair trial or the ability of a public authority to conduct an enquiry of a criminal or disciplinary nature'.

This clause does not seem to include restrictions as practised by the Commission regarding documents pertaining to environmental infringement proceedings.

Finally, I note that Article 255 EC speaks of access to documents of the Commission, Council and EP. I would favour broadening the addressees of this Treaty obligation to all 'organs' and 'institutions' and it should therefore include

---

[18]   Cf. on this Krämer (2003).

[19]   Case T-105/95 *WWF* v. *Commission* [1997] ECR II-313 and Case T-191/99 *Petrie a.o.* v. *Commission* [2001] ECR II-3677.

the Economic and Social Committee, the Committee of the Regions, the European Central Bank etc.

4 Access to the ECJ and CFI[20]

We all know how complicated the admissibility is of ENGOs objecting to EC Directives and Regulations on *environmental* grounds. The reason for all this: the requirement under Article 230 (4) EC of *direct and individual concern*, as it has been interpreted by the ECJ for many years. [21]

The leading 'environmental' case on the admissibility of interested third parties trying to annul decisions affecting the environment is still the *Greenpeace* case.[22]

This case concerned two power stations on the Canary Islands, for which no environmental impact assessment had been prepared. Greenpeace had appealed against a decision of the Court of First Instance.[23] That Court had declared Greenpeace's action seeking annulment of a Commission decision to pay the Spanish Government ECU 12 million from the European Regional Development Fund for the construction of the two power stations inadmissible.

The Court of First Instance had reached this decision referring to the determined case law of the Court of Justice according to which persons other than the addressees may claim that a decision is of direct concern to them only if that decision affects them by reason of certain attributes which are peculiar to them, or by reason of factual circumstances which differentiate them from all other persons and thereby distinguish them individually in the same way as the person addressed.

Accordingly, the CFI held that the criterion proposed by the applicants for appraising their *locus standi*, namely the existence of harm suffered or to be suffered, was not in itself sufficient to confer *locus standi* on an applicant. This was because such harm might affect, in a general abstract way, a large number of persons who could not be determined in advance in such a way as to distin-

---

[20] The relations between ENGOs and the Commission pertaining to infringements of European law by the Member States falls outside the scope of this paper. See on this the Communication of the Commission 'Relations with the Complainant in Respect of Infringements of Community Law'; COM(2002) 141 final and also COM(2002) 725 final /2 'Sur l'amelioration du controle de l'application du droit communautaire'.

[21] Case 25/62 *Plaumann* [1963] ECR 95.

[22] Case C-321/95 P *Greenpeace v. Commission* [1998] ECR I-1651.

[23] Case T-585/93 *Greenpeace v. Commission* [1995] ECR II-2205. Cf. also Case T-117/94 *Associazione Agricoltori della Provincia di Rovigo and Others v. Commission* [1995] ECR II-455 and Case C-142/95 P *Associazione Agricoltori della Provincia di Rovigo and others v. Commission* [1996] ECR I-6669.

guish them individually just like the addressee of a decision, as required under the determined case law mentioned above. There was thus no question of a special regime of *locus standi* in respect of Community environmental decisions, reflecting the public function of the environment.

As far as the *locus standi* of the organization Greenpeace was concerned, the Court of First Instance observed that an association formed for the protection of the collective interests of a category of persons could not be considered to be directly and individually concerned, for the purposes of Article 230 EC, by a measure affecting the general interests of that category, and was therefore not entitled to bring an action for annulment where its members could not do so individually. On appeal the Court of Justice upheld the decision of the Court of First Instance.

The result of this case law of the ECJ is that in general ENGOs do not have *locus standi* at the ECJ to challenge Regulations and Directives.

However, he CFI in the *Jégo-Quéré* case reconsidered its position on the strict interpretation of the notion of 'individual concern' under Article 230 EC and developed a new test to be applied:[24]

> 'a natural or legal person is to be regarded as individually concerned by a Community measure of general application that concerns him directly if the measure in question affects his legal position, in a manner which is both definite and immediate, by restricting his rights or by imposing obligations on him. The number and position of other persons who are likewise affected by the measure, or who may be so, are of no relevance in that regard'.

The new doctrine did not survive for very long. The ECJ delivered judgment in Case C-50/00 P *Unión de Pequeños Agricultores* v. *Council*[25] and this judgment shows that the strict interpretation of 'direct and individual concern' is still very much at the centre of Article 230 (4) EC. *Locus standi* for ENGOs to challenge at the ECJ environmental regulations and directives would require, in the light of the *UPA* judgment, an amendment of the EC Treaty. We suggest that the ECJ's invitation should be followed. Probably the 'easiest' way to bring Article 230 (4) more in line with Article 47 Charter of Fundamental Rights of the European Union and Articles 6 and 13 of the European Convention on Human Rights is to delete the words 'and individual'.

---

[24] Case T-177/01 *Jégo-Quéré* [2002] ECR II-2365.

[25] Case C-50/00 P *Unión de Pequeños Agricultores* v. *Council* [2002] ECR I-6677.

5 Concluding remarks

Many improvements to fostering participatory democracy within the European Union in general and European environmental law in particular can be made within the current Treaty provisions. In many cases it is just a matter of doing 'the right thing' and in others it is sufficient that changes in secondary legislation are made effective.

However, some necessary improvements do require an amendment of the Treaties. It is the author's opinion that:

- the co-decision procedure under Article 175 (1) EC should be the one and only applicable procedure for legislative acts to protect the environment;
- the words 'and individual' in Article 230 (4) EC should be deleted in order to improve legal protection;
- a provision similar to Article 36 of the Preliminary Draft Constitutional Treaty should be inserted in a future Constitutional Treaty in order to ensure that the legislative debates of the European Parliament and of the Council in its legislative form shall be public;
- Article 255 EC should be amended in such a way as to guarantee that access to information from all EU 'organs' and 'institutions' is ensured.

CHAPTER 5

The EC's External Competence and the Protection of the Environment

Massimiliano Montini

1   Introduction

The issue of the boundaries of the EC's external competence has always given rise to extensive debates between EC law scholars.[1] Furthermore, the European Court of Justice has been called upon in several cases to decide on the subject and has provided the EC institutions and the interpreters with some principles which nowadays constitute the operative tools by which to better address and solve on a case by case basis such complex issues as the demarcation of powers between the EC institutions and the Member States in the external sphere.

It has been rightly noted by Dashwood that when dealing with the issue of the EC's external competence, two important questions of principle arise: the 'existence question' and the 'exclusivity question'.[2] Both issues relate to the division and demarcation of powers in the external sphere between the European Community and the Member States and require a preliminary examination in the context of the present contribution, insofar as they represent the framework structure of the EC's external competence. Therefore, these questions will be the object of our analysis in the first part of the present paper.

However, the EC's external competence in the environmental sphere also has a specific nature and should not be underestimated. This is due to various reasons, which will be better addressed in the second part of the present paper. After a general and brief survey of the reasons for such a specific nature, the focus of our analysis in the final part of this contribution will then be placed on the issue of the relationship between the EC's external policy in the field of environmental protection and the possibly conflicting obligations arising from the GATT and other multilateral conventions for the regulation and promotion of international trade administered by the World Trade Organization.

2   The existence question

The existence question arises from the combined effect of the two following features of the EC legal order:

(1)   the presence of the principle of attribution of powers, according to which the European Community enjoys normative competence only in those sectors and insofar as such competence has been explicitly attributed to it by the EC Treaty or other relevant sources of EC law;

---

[1]   See in general MacLeod (1996); McGoldrick (1997); Koskenniemi (1998); Gaja (1999), at 139 *et seq.*; Dashwood & Hillion (2000).

[2]   See Dashwood (1998), at 113 *et seq.*; see also Dashwood & Heliskoski (2000) and Dashwood (2000a).

(2)   the absence of a 'parallel' between the internal and the external competence attributed by the Treaty to the EC institutions.

The text of the original 1957 EC Treaty contained just a few provisions on the
competence of the EC in external relations. A specific external relations competence was in fact only provided in the fields of commercial policy (see Article 133
EC) and for association agreements with third countries (see Article 310 EC).
Later, with the 1986 European Single Act and the 1992 Maastricht Treaty, a
specific EC external competence was introduced in other fields, among which is
the field of environmental protection (see Article 174 (4) EC):

>   'Within their respective spheres of competence, the Community and the Member
>   States shall cooperate with third countries and with the competent international
>   organisations. The arrangements for Community cooperation may be the subject of
>   agreements between the Community and the third parties concerned, which shall be
>   negotiated and concluded in accordance with Article 300'.

However, in many sectors the European Community still lacks an *explicit* external competence. The following question therefore arises: can the EC's external
competence in a certain sector be inferred by the existence of a corresponding
internal competence in the same field?
    There is no general and consistently valid answer to the question raised
above. However, the case law and the several opinions delivered by the ECJ on
the matter have contributed to highlighting a series of principles and guidelines which can be used by the interpreter to ascertain whether or not the EC
institutions have external competence in a given sector. Such principles may be
summarised as follows.

(1) The principle of the attribution of powers
    The principle of the attribution of powers, as stated in Article 5 EC, accord-
ing to which 'The Community shall act within the limits of the powers
conferred upon it by this Treaty and of the objectives assigned to it therein'. Such
a principle states in clear terms what is immanent in the EC legal order, that
is that the European Community enjoys a normative competence only in those
sectors and to the extent to which it has been explicitly conferred with powers by
the EC Treaty or other relevant sources of EC law. The principle of the attribution of powers is supplemented by the principles of subsidiarity and proportionality which limit the concrete exercise of the EC competence in order to protect
the prerogatives of the Member States, once the Community competence has
been ascertained.

(2) The principle of the absence of a parallel between the EC's internal and external competence

The main consequence of this principle is the fact that once the existence of the EC competence in a certain sector has been ascertained it does not automatically follow that the Community also enjoys an external competence in the same sector. On the contrary, in general terms pursuant to the general principles of the Community legal order such an external competence should normally be explicit, that is it should be explicitly provided by EC Treaty provisions, with the exception of the situations covered by the two principles created by ECJ case law, namely the 'implied external powers principle' and the 'effectiveness principle'.

(3) The 'implied external powers principle

The 'implied external powers principle' states that the Community must not always base its external competence on explicit EC Treaty provisions (although this is the normal situation), as in some cases such a competence may be implicitly inferred from other provisions of the Treaty, pursuant to Article 308 EC. This principle was first affirmed by the ECJ, although not in very clear terms, in the *ERTA* case (1971).[3] This case, which arose out of a dispute over the Community's competence to sign the European Road Transport Agreement, is best known for its contribution to the development of the 'exclusivity principle', which I will examine in the next section. However, a careful reading of paragraph 17 of the ECJ's decision in the *ERTA* case shows that it contains the first implicit affirmation of the 'implied external powers principle', as noted by Dashwood.[4] Paragraph 17 of the *ERTA* case states:

> *'In particular, each time the Community, with a view to implementing a common policy envisaged by the Treaty , adopts provisions laying down common rules, whatever form they may take, the Member States no longer have the right, acting individually or even collectively, to under take obligations with third countries which affect those rules.'*

The reasoning of the Court in the *ERTA* case, however, while implicitly admitting the possibility to infer the existence of a Community external competence from the existence of an internal competence, nevertheless seemed to limit such a possibility to the situation where the said internal competence had been concretely exercised. In other words, the decision of the ECJ in the *ERTA* case left a certain question open. The question was whether an implied EC's external competence may arise in a situation in which the corresponding internal competence has yet not been exercised.

---

[3]   See Case 22/70 *Commission v. Council (ERTA* case) [1971] ECR 263.

[4]   See Dashwood (1998), at 118.

Such a question was first answered by the ECJ, once again not in very clear terms, in the 1976 *Kramer* case,[5] which dealt with the EC's versus Member States' competence in the field of the conservation of marine resources. In this case, the Court affirmed that although the Community had no internal legislation in place in the field of the conservation of marine resources, based on the fact that, according to EC law, on an internal level the EC institutions had the power to take any measures directed towards the conservation of the biological resources of the sea, it naturally followed that the Community similarly had the power to conclude international agreements for the conservation of marine resources. See in this respect in particular paragraph 33 of the *Kramer* case, which affirms that:

'*It follows from the very duties and powers which Community law has established and assigned to the institutions of the Community on the internal level that the Community has authority to enter into international commitments for the conservation of the resources of the sea*'

In the later case law of the ECJ, the 'implied external powers principle' was reiterated in various other situations.[6] Moreover, its extent was then reinforced by the 'effectiveness principle', first affirmed by the Court in *Opinion 1/76*.

(4) The 'effectiveness principle' or the 'necessary attainment principle'
The 'effectiveness principle' or the 'necessary attainment principle' was first affirmed by the ECJ in *Opinion 1/76*,[7] dealing with the EC's competence to conclude an International Agreement establishing an European laying-up fund for inland waterway vessels. It states that whenever Community law has internally created certain powers for the institutions of the Community for the purpose of attaining a specific objective, the Community then has the authority to enter into international commitments even in the absence of an explicit provision to this effect contained in the text of the Treaty, and even if the corresponding internal power has yet not been exercised by the Community institutions, whenever '*the participation of the Community in the international agreement is necessary for the attainment of one the objectives of the Community*'.[8]
The 'effectiveness principle' or the 'necessary attainment principle' was subsequently reiterated by the ECJ in similar terms in various other cases, among which *Opinion 2/94* has a paramount role.[9] It dealt with the proposal

---

5   See Joined Cases 3, 4, 6/76 *Kramer* [1976] ECR 1279.

6   See for instance Opinion 1/76, § 3, and Opinion 2/94, § 25, cited below.

7   See Opinion 1/76 [1977] ECR 741.

8   See paras. 3-4 of Opinion 1/76.

9   See Opinion 2/94 [1996] ECR I-1759. See also more recent the judgments of the ECJ on the so called 'Open Sky' Agreements, e.g. Case C-476/98 *Commission* v. *Germany*, judgment of 5 November 2002, not yet reported in the ECR, paras. 80 *et seq.*

for the EC to accede to the European Convention on Human Rights. In such a circumstance, the Court recalled in very clear terms that whenever the EC Treaty confers specific internal powers on the EC institutions in order to attain a certain objective, 'the Community is empowered to enter into the international commitments necessary for attainment of that objective even in the absence of an express provision to that effect'.[10]

In other words, from the ECJ case law on the 'effectiveness principle' or the 'necessary attainment principle' it can be inferred that when the attainment of a certain objective laid down in the EC Treaty could be seriously imperilled when the Community merely acts internally, but not externally, it appears to be more effective to recognise specific external powers of the EC institutions in the sector concerned, even in the absence of any explicit EC Treaty provision in this sense.

Now that we have briefly described the principles which have been developed by the ECJ case law to address what we have referred to as the 'existence question', let us now proceed to an analysis of the so-called 'exclusivity question', which may occur only when the existence question has been resolved.

3   The exclusivity question

Once in a material case the exclusivity question has been addressed and resolved, that is once the interpreter has been able to conclude that the Community enjoys external legislative competence in a given case, the 'exclusivity issue' arises. The exclusivity issue, that is the issue of whether the Community enjoys exclusive competence with respect to the powers possibly pertaining to the Member States, can obviously only arise in those fields in which the Community enjoys a 'concurrent competence' with that of the Member States. In fact, if in a certain field, such as in common commercial policy or more precisely in the trade in goods sector, the Community enjoys an exclusive internal and external competence *per se*, then the exclusivity issue obviously has no role to play.[11] The problem instead arises in those cases in which the Community has a competence which is concurrent with those of the Member States and the boundaries between their respective roles and powers are not entirely clear.

---

[10] See para. 26 of Opinion 2/94.

[11] See on the issue of the demarcation between common commercial policy and environmental protection Case C-281/01 *Commission v. Council*, judgment of 12 December 2002, not yet reported in the ECR and Opinion 2/00 on the Cartagena Protocol [2001] ECR I-9713. Cf. also Jans (2000), Chapter II.

In order to address the exclusivity issue in a nutshell, some principles derived from the EC case law on the matter may be of certain assistance. These principles are:
- the *exclusivity* principle and
- the *loyalty* principle.

The *exclusivity principle* originates from the ECJ judgment delivered in the 1971 *ERTA* case. The principle is contained in paragraphs 17 and 22 of the judgment. In particular, in paragraph 17 the ECJ confirmed that once the Community has laid down 'common rules', with a view to implementing a common policy envisaged in the EC Treaty, the Member States no longer have the right, neither individually nor collectively, to undertake obligations with third countries which may 'affect' those common rules.[12] The exclusivity principle in fact creates a parallel between internal competence, when it has been concretely exercised by the Community through the adoption of common rules, and the relative external competence. The same concept is also re-affirmed in similar terms in paragraph 22 of the judgment, which states:

'To the extent to which Community rules are promulgated for the attainment of the objectives of the Treaty, the Member States cannot, outside the framework of the Community institutions, assume obligations which might affect those rules or alter their scope'.[13]

The exclusivity principle was then reiterated by the Court in *Opinion 1/76* and further refined in *Opinion 1/94*,[14] which dealt with the EC's competence to conclude the 1994 WTO Agreement and the related multilateral commercial agreements. In such a case, in particular, the Court seemed to clarify and somehow limit the extent of the principle by stating that:

'The Member States, whether acting individually or collectively, only lose their right to assume obligations with non-member countries as and when common rules which could be affected by those obligations come into being'.[15]

The *loyalty principle*, enshrined in Article 10 EC, states that the Member States must abstain from every behaviour which may forfeit their obligations arising from the EC Treaty or secondary Community legislation. In the present context, on the basis of the 'loyalty principle', Member States should refrain from under-

---

[12]   See para. 17 of the *ERTA* case, cited above at note 4.

[13]   See para. 22 of the *ERTA* case.

[14]   See Opinion 1/94 [1994] ECR I-5267.

[15]   See para. 77 of Opinion 1/94.

taking international obligations, not only in those sectors which fall within the sphere of the Community's common policies established by the EC Treaty, but also in every other possible legislative sector.

It follows from the above that once the Community has adopted common rues within a specific sector, Member States must abstain from adopting rules which may affect them. However, what does it mean to 'affect' such common rules in concrete terms?

It may be derived from the ECJ case law that a distinction can be made between cases when the Community legislation has achieved complete harmonisation and cases when it has simply set some minimum standards.[16] In the former case, in fact, when the Community has adopted legislation which provides an exhaustive regulation of a certain matter on an internal level, it follows from the ECJ case law that the Community enjoys exclusive competence in the matter, also on an external level. In such a case, therefore, the enactment of EC legislation which has achieved complete harmonisation on an internal level pre-empts the adoption of either internal or external measures by the Member States.[17] Conversely, when the Community has adopted internal legislation which simply sets minimum standards, rather than achieving complete harmonisation, in principle the Member States still retain the power to undertake international obligations and to conclude international agreements which set higher standards. In such a case, in fact, the Community and the Member States maintain a concurrent external competence.[18]

4   The specific situation in the environmental field

Keeping in mind the general remarks on the distribution of the external competence between the Community and the Member States which have been made above, it is now time to address the specific situation in the environmental field, which in many respects presents some distinct and specific features.[19]

First of all, in the environmental sector there is no problem regarding the 'existence question' examined above, at least since the introduction of a specific provision on the EC's external competence in this sector, which occurred together which the introduction of the general 'Title on the Environment' in the EC Treaty. This took place under the 1986 Single European Act. The relevant provision, namely Article 174 (4) EC, in fact explicitly states that, within their

---

[16] See O'Keeffe (2000).

[17] See for instance paras. 17-18 of the *ERTA* case and para. 96 of Opinion 1/94.

[18] See for instance paras. 18-21 of Opinion 2/91(*Opinion on ILO Convention*) [1993] ECR I-1061.

[19] See in general Chalmers (1998); Jans (2000), at 69 *et seq.*; Thieme (2001); Loibl (2002).

respective spheres of competence, the Community and the Member States are empowered to conclude agreements with third countries and international organisations.

Secondly, as to the exclusivity question, in the environmental field the European Community may adopt internal provisions which either amount to complete harmonisation or which merely set minimum standards. On the basis of what we have said above, it should be stated that in the former case the Member States are prevented from exercising any form of external competence, whereas in the latter case the parallel existence of a concurrent Community and Member State external competence is indeed possible. In concrete terms, therefore, when the Community has not fully harmonised a certain matter in the environmental sector, the Member States retain the possibility to undertake international obligations independently from the adoption of similar or different external actions by the EC institutions.

Having said that, the following question immediately arises: are there any limits to the conclusion of such external agreements by the Member States? The wording of Article 174(4) EC suggests that no specific limits are imposed by the provision in question as regards the concurrent external competence of the Member States in the environmental field. Therefore, the only limits posed by the EC legal order on the power of the Member States to act in such cases are represented by the general limitation which is inherent to the EC Treaty, and which is enshrined in the 'loyalty principle'. According to this principle, contained in Article 10 EC, Member States must refrain from behaving in a way which may run counter the fulfilment of their obligations under Community law or which may undermine the effectiveness of such obligations.

In practice, however, in the environmental field the conflict between international obligations undertaken by the Community and other international obligations independently undertaken by the Member States is not likely to occur. Quite on the contrary, with regard to the most important contemporary environmental issues, the Community and the Member States have often chosen to opt for the conclusion of 'mixed agreements'. Such agreements are together negotiated by the Community and the Member States, signed and ratified separately but in a co-ordinated way by the Community and the Member States and jointly executed within the framework of their respective competence.[20]

The conclusion of 'mixed agreements' is generally to be appreciated insofar as it constitutes a particular way of exercising the concurrent competence which limits, to the minimum, the risk of undertaking different and conflicting obligations by the Community and Member States in the same matter. Having said this, however, is the conclusion of mixed agreements totally free from any shortcomings? The answer to this question is probably no. In fact, the practice

---

[20] On the topic see Rosas (2000).

of mixed agreements, although quite successful and effective, particularly in the environmental field, raises various questions which can be summarised as follows:

- In the conclusion, adoption and implementation of mixed agreements in the environmental sector where is the effective centre of power? Does it lie in the hands of the Community or in those of the Member States?
- When the conclusion of international agreements pre-empts and/or substitutes the adoption of internal legislation by the EC institutions, there may be a problem of 'democracy' for the EC legal order, insofar as the procedure for the adoption of international agreement by the Community, contained in Article 300 EC, only foresees a limited competence for the European Parliament and places the 'political' power in the hands of the Commission and the 'legal' power in the hands of the Council.
- Mixed agreements also raise the issue of the respective international responsibility of the Community and the Member States. In very general terms, under a mixed agreement both the Community and the Member States concerned are jointly responsible at the international level for the non-fulfilment of the obligations arising from the said agreement.[21] However, with their instrument of ratification or accession to an international agreement the Community and the Member States may clearly state the scope of their respective competence, thus also clarifying the scope of their respective responsibility.[22] Moreover, under Community law, an internal 'agreement' between the EC institutions and the Member States may sometimes be signed in order to better define their respective competence and to apportion the consequent responsibility under international law.[23]
- The issue of the international responsibility of the Community and its Member States may also be related to the issue of the responsibility of

---

[21] See for instance Article 4(6) of the Kyoto Protocol on Climate Change (available at www.unfccc.de), which establishes, in accordance with Article 24(2) of the same Protocol, that the Community and the Member States are jointly responsible for the fulfilment by the Community of its commitments under the Protocol.

[22] See for instance the Declaration by the European Community made in accordance with Article 24(3) of the Kyoto Protocol which determines the respective spheres of competence of the Community and its Member States in the field of environmental protection. The Declaration is annexed to Council Decision 2002/358 of 25 April 2002 on the approval on behalf of the European Community of the Kyoto Protocol, published in OJ 2002, L 130/1.

[23] See for instance the Intergovernmental Agreement reached by the EC Member States' Environmental Ministers on the contribution of each Member State to the overall commitment assigned to the European Community by the Kyoto Protocol, Doc. 9702/98 of 19 June 1998 of the Council of the European Union.

the Members States towards the Community under EC law. In fact, if a Member State fails to fulfil its obligations under a mixed agreement to which both the Community and the Members States are Parties and such a violation also results in a violation of the agremeents' obligations by the European Community, then the Member State in question, besides its international responsibility towards the other Parties to the agreement, also bears responsibility towards the Community under EC Law.

5 The EC's external competence and the WTO obligations

Now that we have examined the issue of the distribution of external competence between the Community and the Member States in the environmental sector, it is now time to address the 'hottest' issue which pertains to such a division of competence. This is the issue of the relationship between the EC's external policy in the field of environmental protection and the possibly conflicting obligations arising from the GATT and the other multilateral conventions for the regulation and promotion of international trade, administered by the World Trade Organization.

As a preliminary remark, it should be underlined that the WTO Agreement and all the multilateral commercial agreements signed under the auspices of the WTO are mixed agreements to which both the Community and the Member States are Parties and that while the Agreements bind the Community under international law, the Member States are bound by them both under international law towards third Parties and under EC law towards the Community, pursuant to Article 300 (7) EC.

Having said this, before starting on an analysis of the provisions pertaining to 'trade and environment',[24] it should first be recalled that the multilateral trading regime does not in principle rule out the possibility for the Parties to the GATT and to other commercial agreements to afford adequate protection to their environmental interests under certain conditions, although it is a generally accepted principle in the field of international environmental law that

'unilateral actions to deal with environmental problems should be avoided and environmental measures addressing transboundary or global environmental problems should, as far as possible, be based on international consensus'.[25]

---

[24] For a general overview on the 'trade and environment' issue see for instance Wiers (2002); Cameron (1994); Esty (1994); Petersmann (1995); Francioni (2001).

[25] See Principle 12 of the 1992 Rio Declaration.

In other words, the Parties should pursue their environmental policies at the international level preferably only by means of accession to Multilateral Environmental Agreements. However, a quick look at international practice shows that this is not the case and while MEAs are not absent from the international arena (see for instance the 1989 Basle Convention on transboundary movement of hazardous waste, the 1985 Vienna Convention of the protection of the ozone layer or the 1992 Framework Convention on Climate Change, as supplemented by the related Protocols), they are generally less frequent than unilateral environmental measures taken at the national level by the GATT Parties.

As far as the Community and its Member States are concerned, it should be highlighted that 'unilateral' environmental measures which 'discriminate' against imported products are usually taken both at the Community level, with respect to measures falling within the category of 'trade-related environmental measures', such as, for instance, those prohibiting the import, sale and use within the Community territory of meat deriving form cattle treated with hormones,[26] and at the Member State level, with respect to purely national measures aimed at the protection of the environment or the health and safety of citizens or workers, such as, for instance, those taken to prevent the accidental contamination of citizens and workers which may be caused by asbestos fibres which formed the basis of the French ban on Canadian imported asbestos and products containing asbestos.[27]

Once the Community or a Member State takes an unilateral measure aimed at the protection of the environment outside their territory, the issue of the compatibility of such an unilateral environmental measure with its obligations under the GATT and other multilateral commercial agreements arises. In the present context, let us limit our analysis to the GATT provisions. In this sense, it can be said that the basic principle upon which the GATT is based is the principle of non-discrimination which is enshrined in:

- the 'most-favoured nation' clause (MFN clause), according to which all tariff concessions accorded to one State must be automatically extended to all other GATT Contracting Parties (GATT Article I).
- The 'national treatment' clause (NT clause), on the basis of which imported goods, once they have entered into the national market of a given State, must not be subject to less favourable treatment than national products (GATT Article III).
- In addition to the above two clauses, the principle of non-discrimination is completed by the provision of GATT Article XI, which prohibits all quantitative or similar restrictions on imported products other than tariffs.

---

[26] See the *Hormones case*, WTO Appellate Body Report, WT/DS26-DS48/AB/R, 16 January 1998.

[27] See the *Asbestos case*, WTO Appellate Body Report, WT/DS135/AB/R, 12 March 2001.

The norms just mentioned, taken together, are aimed at promoting a freer and fairer global trade with the ultimate goal of furthering economic growth through the expansion of international trade. In such a legal regime, obviously the freedom of trade is the main objective and the main concern. However, this does not mean that international trade must remain unrestricted in all circumstances. The GATT Treaty itself contemplates some cases in which trade can be legitimately restricted to afford adequate protection to important interests of the Contracting Parties, provided that certain requirements are met. The main reasons which a State can invoke in order to limit the free flow of international trade are those listed in Article XX of the GATT under the heading of 'general exceptions'.

According to GATT Article XX, the burden imposed on trade by unilateral measures taken by a Contracting Party with the aim of protecting one of the interests listed therein, can be considered to be compatible with the GATT rules provided that, pursuant to the *chapeau* of Article XX, *'such measures are not applied in a manner which would constitute a means of arbitrary or unjustifiable discrimination between countries where the same conditions prevail, or a disguised restriction on international trade'*. As regards environmental protection in particular, among the several exceptions which may justify a limitation to the unrestricted flow of international trade contained in Article XX, two of them play an important role. They are:

- Article XX(b) which deals with the national measures *'necessary to protect human, animal or plant life or health'*; and
- Article XX(g) which refers to the national measures *'relating to the conservation of exhaustible natural resources, if such measures are made effective in conjunction with restriction on domestic production or consumption'.*

In other words, since the GATT does not include an explicit reference to the 'environment' as such, national measures taken by the Parties and which are aimed at environmental protection have been justified under either Article XX(b) or XX(g). Leaving aside in the present context the analysis of the operative and concrete issues regarding the correct method of applying the exceptions contained in GATT Article XX, let us now briefly comment on the 'extraterritoriality' issue, which emerges within the framework of the trade and environment question.

The extraterritoriality issue should be framed in the following way. Considering that it becomes apparent from the principles and the basic rules governing international trade under the WTO legal order that the common commercial rules agreed upon at international level do not in principle exclude the possibility for the Parties to give priority under specific circumstances to environmental

---

[28] See the *Tuna/Dolphin I case*, GATT Panel Report, reproduced at 30 ILM 1594.

objectives as opposed to trade goals, but at the same time the adoption of internationally agreed standards should be generally preferred to recourse to unilateral measures, is it possible to envisage under the GATT a power for the Parties
to adopt unilateral measures with an extraterritorial reach?

In this respect, it should be very briefly noted that the GATT/WTO case law
in recent years has been characterised by the progressive departure from a very
restrictive approach,[28] according to which any kind of unilateral measure taken
by a Party for the protection of the environment outside its territory should be
considered impermissible under GATT Article XX, to a more open-minded and
flexible approach which has firstly recognised the theoretical possibility of the
extraterritorial application of an unilateral measure taken by a Party,[29] and then
explicitly accepted the possibility that the Parties adopt unilateral measures with
an extraterritorial scope in certain specific situations, such as for the protection
of migratory species.[30]

As regards EC environmental policy in particular, it should be noted that
while the EC institutions have been stating on several occasions that in principle they prefer to achieve general objectives relating to the protection of
the environment through forms of co-ordinated and concerted actions at the
international level rather than by unilateral measures, in practice they have
often adopted unilateral measures for the protection of the environment, some
of which have been explicitly held to be incompatible with the GATT obligations,
such as those on the ban on meat derived from cattle treated with hormones[31]
and many others, although not judicially considered, may probably be held to
be not in conformity with the GATT obligations (see for instance the ban on
furs from animals taken by means of leghold traps,[32] the ban on the import of
cetacean products for commercial purposes,[33] the ban on the import of skins of
seal pups[34] or the regulation voluntarily implementing the CITES Convention's
provisions[35]).

In sum, therefore, it should be concluded that up to now it is not completely
clear to what extent unilateral measures adopted by GATT Parties, including the
EC, to pursue environmental objectives may be held to be compatible with the
WTO rules on international trade. There is probably no set answer in general
terms, but an appropriate balance must be found on a case by case basis, with

---

[29] See the *Tuna/ Dolphin II case*, GATT Panel Report, 1994, reproduced at 33 ILM 274.

[30] See *Shrimps/Turtles I case*, WTO Appellate Body Report, WT/DS58/AB/R, 6 November 1998.

[31] See the *Hormones case*, cited above.

[32] See Regulation 3254/91, OJ 1991, L 308/1.

[33] See Regulation 348/81, OJ L 1981, 39/1.

[34] See Directive 83/129, as amended by Directive 89/370, OJ 1989, L 163/37.

[35] See Regulation 338/97, OJ 1997, L 61/1.

[36] See Montini (2001).

recourse to the balancing tool represented by the 'necessity principle', as developed in the GATT/WTO case law in the 'trade and environment' sphere.[36]

A final question pertaining to the issue of the unilateral adoption of national measures to achieve environmental protection objectives concerns the possibility to envisage a 'special' regime for those multilateral or national measures aiming to protect the 'global environment'. In such a case, unfortunately, as yet there is no general international practice available which can support the conclusion that a 'special regime' is required in order to evaluate the compatibility of such measures with the multilateral trading rules, although the specific nature and the special importance of some of the most urgent global environmental issues, such as ozone depletion or climate change, would probably deserve new and more courageous approaches in this sense.

CHAPTER 6

The Future Role of the ECJ in the Development of European Environmental Law

Ludwig Krämer*

1 Introduction: the environment and the future

Any reflection on the future role of the Court of Justice in the
development of environmental law is influenced by speculation, as is the case
with any statement about the future. At best, attempts may be made to sketch
the Court's role in the past and to try to prudently prolong this impression
into the future, taking into account the evolution of the state of the European
environment, the future development of environmental law, the future political, economic, social and environmental integration of Europe and the future of
integrating environmental requirements into the global economy.

The assumption is that the European and global legal evolution in environmental matters up to the year 2020 will be marked by the following features,
although the attributed space does not allow one to elaborate upon them:

- global environmental law will continue to provide for rules which are
  hardly enforceable and which are not enforced, as they are too general, they
  offer too many exceptions and do not seriously put into question the principle of national sovereignty;
- the United States will continue, as in the past twenty years, to prevent the
  development of effective provisions of international environmental law and
  will continue to promote, instead, international trade and economic development; its influence on the (non-)development of environmental law will
  remain overwhelming;
- the European Union will not be able to generally assume a steering position in the development of global environmental law; it will continue to
  be occupied with the solution of the numerous problems involved in the
  enlargement of the European Union and their impact on the environment;
  the Union's potential lies in the development of European regional law
  provisions;
- environmental law-making within the European Union will develop more
  framework legislation, more general legal provisions and more basic rules
  – such as the need to ensure sustainable development, to integrate environmental requirements into all policies, to follow certain environmental principles, to ensure a high level of environmental protection etc. – which allow
  efficient environmental protection, if there is sufficient political will, but
  which will also allow environmental requirements to be neglected, if other
  priorities prevail. As the judicial self-restraint on the part of the Court of
  Justice quite rightly puts into question the legislature's decision only in
  extreme cases, there will be less judicial challenges to standard-setting and
  enforcement;

---

*   The author only expresses his personal opinion.

- enforcement will remain the most important aspect of environmental law; however, as the precision of environmental rules will decrease, enforcement will lose part of its actuality: up until now, it has not been possible for instance to enforce 'sustainable development', to stop the progressive disappearance of species of fauna and flora or to enforce the application of environmental requirements in transport policy and law. And this tendency is not likely to change.

2 The Court of Justice and the protection of the environment in the past

The Court of Justice's record in environmental matters over the last twenty-five years is almost entirely positive. Of the 306 environmental judgments[1] delivered up to the end of 2002, there might be half a dozen where one could have the impression that considerations of policy had determined the outcome more than the protection of the environment. I count among these the judgments on French traditional hunting methods[2], the Belgian import ban on waste[3], the Danish bottles case[4] and, from recent times, the Greenpeace case of the Canaries[5] and the Finnish energy tax case.[6]

In contrast, however, there are numerous cases where the Court's decision sided with the environment and against other interests which were protected by the EU Treaty. A detailed presentation of such cases which are relatively frequent in the area of trade in goods, eco-taxes and generally in those areas where EC law leaves some room for national legislatures, is not possible here.[7] The weighing of environmental interests against other interests which the EC Treaty requires in several provisions, has become one of the marked features of the Court's jurisdiction over the last two decades. It is necessary to mention this aspect in particular, as the Court has undoubtedly made extensive use of the possibilities offered by the EC Treaty, sometimes with rather innovative legal constructions. However, striking such a balance is often forgotten or neglected, when new EC legislation is being enacted or when the question of whether there

---

[1] This number is based on my own accounts; see for details Krämer (2002a), 483 with reference to earlier publications. This number is somewhat arbitrary, as in particular in internal market issues, transport, energy or tax law opinions differ as to what constitutes an 'environmental' case.

[2] Case C-252/85 *Commission* v. *France* [1988] ECR 2243.

[3] Case C-2/90 *Commission* v. *Belgium* [1992] ECR I-4431.

[4] Case C-302/86 *Commission* v. *Denmark* [1988] ECR 4607.

[5] Case C-321/97 *Greenpeace* [1998] ECR I-1651.

[6] Case C-213/96 *Outokumpu Oy* [1998] ECR I-1777.

[7] See for more details Krämer (2002) and the reference in note 1.

should be new EC legislation is being discussed. With regard to the environment, negative integration still prevails in the European Union and the argument that between the strong and the weak, negative integration oppresses and
positive integration has a freeing effect[8], does not determine the EU's (environmental) policy. It is unlikely that this will change in the future.

It follows from all this that past jurisdiction gives no reason to doubt the
Court's capacity to efficiently put into practice the EC Treaty's requirement that
the environment must be protected at a high level, and that also in the future
the interpretation of secondary environmental law will be appropriately dealt
with by the Court.

3 Trends for the future

By the year 2020, there will be many more Member States in
the Union than the present fifteen and the ten countries, which will accede by
2004. Future enlargements will include Romania, Bulgaria and the Balkan
countries, possibly also Turkey, Belarus, Ukraine and other states. The accession of Russia which is certainly as much a European State as Turkey, cannot
be excluded, unless the political will to build a true European Union with a
common foreign and defence policy leads to corresponding political and institutional steps.

This may be so: the evolution is likely to lead to a considerable increase in
the number of judges. At present, there is one judge per Member State at the
Court of Justice and 'at least one judge' per Member State at the Court of First
Instance. It is likely that any future EU Member State will have one judge at
both the Court of Justice and the Court of First Instance. This will make the
sitting of the full Court – which is already at present restricted to cases of a
disciplinary nature – even less frequent and thus the coherence of EC law less
easy. The different chambers of the Court and the Grand Chamber will lead to,
with their increased number and the different legal, institutional and economic
backgrounds of the judges, greater difficulties in ensuring consistency among
themselves and as regards the European jurisdiction generally.

Divergence trends are likely to increase with the possibility to create 'judicial
panels', in order 'to hear and determine at first instance certain classes of action
or proceedings brought in specific cases'.[9] Such panels may first be established
for staff matters, questions of Community industrial property rights[10] and
perhaps competition law; however, it is rather unlikely that access to justice as

---

[8] Paraphrasing La Rochfoucauld: *'Entre le fort et le faible, c'est la liberté qui oppresse et c'est la loi qui libère'.*

[9] Articles 220(2) and 225a EC, inserted by the Treaty of Nice.

[10] See in this regard Article 229a EC, inserted by the Treaty of Nice.

regards environmental acts or omissions by Community institutions and other bodies will be conferred on such panels, even after the adoption of the relevant proposal for an EC regulation on the application of the principles of the Aarhus Convention to EC institutions. The reason for this is that environmental requirements form an integrated part of all EC policies (Article 6 EC) which rather advocates against the establishment of specialised courts or chambers for such a horizontal objective. Indeed, it will be difficult to consider a case on national eco taxes, on the banning of a certain substance or a product or on marine pollution as an environmental case and not as a tax, trade or transport case.

A further element of uncertainty for the future is the possibility for the Council to create Assistant Rapporteurs who are 'to participate in preparatory inquiries in cases pending before the Court and to cooperate with the Judge who acts as Rapporteur'.[11] These Assistant Rapporteurs are likely to play an important role in particular in cases where the Judge Rapporteur does not know the language of the affected Member State, a situation which is likely to be rather frequent in the future, in particular as regards accession countries.

To date, the current EC provisions do not provide the possibility for judicial decisions to be taken by a single judge, except in cases of interim measures under Article 243 EC. In view of the difficult integration of the legal cultures of EC Member States, it appears to be a wise political decision to have chambers of at least three judges of, by definition, different nationality to deliver judgments. This is likely to diminish the risk of decisions being appealed. In the past, the nationality of a judge or the absence of a judge with the same nationality as one of the parties[12] never appeared to have played any role in judicial environmental matters.

The division of work between national courts and Community courts in the enforcement of judgements has remained unchanged since the EC Treaty in 1958. The interpretation of EC law is a matter for the European court. The national courts may ask the Court of Justice for its interpretation of EC law and, where their judgments can no longer be appealed under national law, they are obliged to ask the Court for a preliminary ruling (Article 234 EC). For a number of years, the Commission has published cases where it is of the opinion that a national supreme court has been obliged, in the Commission's opinion, to submit a case to the Court of Justice for a preliminary judgment, but has not done so.[13] This publication is not complete: it only refers to supreme courts, not to other national courts the judgments of which cannot be appealed, and it is selective in its choice of cases. In no case has the Commission brought an action against a Member State because a national court has disregarded the requirements of Article 234. Environmental law does not make any exception to these rules.

---

[11] Article 13 of the Protocol on the Statute of the Court of Justice, OJ 2001, C 80/53.

[12] Such reasons may not be invoked before the Courts, see Articles 18 (4) and 47 of the Statute (note 11).

Between 1976 and 2002, the Court delivered 69 preliminary judgments
in environmental cases[14] which constitute about 2.5% of all preliminary cases
that were decided by the Court. This confirms the general impression that,
in matters of EC environmental law, the facts of the case are frequently not in
dispute. The parties more often argue on different evaluation of the facts or
balancing the different interests at stake.

More generally, environmental cases which were decided by the Court of
Justice were marked by a number of features:

- More than 60 percent (195 out of 306) of the cases are based on Article 226
  EC where the Commission alone is entitled to initiate proceedings;
- The enforcement of environmental law by one Member State against the
  other, foreseen in Article 227 EC, is theoretical: no such case has ever been
  brought before the Court;
- The procedure before the Court under Article 226 is preceded by a pre-litigation procedure between the Commission and the Member States. More
  than 90 percent of all environmental procedures initiated under Article
  226 end before the matter is decided by the Court of Justice;[15]
- The procedure under Article 226 takes, on average, 59 months, almost five
  years; 38 months are used for the pre-litigation stage, 21 months for the
  court procedure.[16]

In order to remedy these difficulties, at least in part, the Convention, as
suggested by the Commission, is considering a new European Treaty or better
a European Constitution, to again to include a provision similar to Article 88
ECSC (not longer in force), according to which the Commission should finally

---

[13] These findings are published in part in the annex to the Commission's annual reports on monitoring
the application of Community law, see, for instance, 16th Annual Report (1998), OJ 1999, C 354/1 at
184; 17th Annual Report (1999), OJ 2001, C 30/1 at 192; 18th Annual Report (2000), COM (2001) 309
of 16 July 2001, annex VI.

[14] See Krämer (2002a); most cases were referred to the Court by Italian (20), Dutch (13) and French (9)
courts. No preliminary judgments had been rquested up to the end of 2001 by courts from Greece,
Ireland, Portugal and Spain.

[15] In 1999 the Commission sent 1075 letters of formal notice to the Member States and in 178 cases
appealed to the Court. In 40 cases, the application was later withdrawn or the case was otherwise
settled. In 2000, 1317 letters of formal notice were sent, and 172 applications were made to the Court,
out of which 105 were later withdrawn or otherwise settled. In 2001 1050 letters of formal notice were
sent and 162 applications were made, out of which 75 were later withdrawn or otherwise settled. Figures
from the Commission, Monitoring the application of Community law, 17th report (note 13); 18th report
(2000) (note 13), vol. II tables 2.1 and 2.5; 19th report (2001), COM (2002) 324 of 28 June 2002, ann. II,
tables 2.2 and 2.5. There are no separate figures for environmental cases.

[16] See Krämer (2002a).

decide on any breach of EC law by a Member State. The Member State should then be entitled to appeal to the Court of Justice against the Commission's decision.

This procedure would probably make the application to the Court of Justice superfluous in a number of cases, in particular where Member States have not transposed EC directives into national law, or where such transposition has been incomplete or incorrect.[17] Indeed, these cases – when it really comes to a judgment by the Court – are almost always won by the Commission, and the infringement of EC law is hardly ever in dispute: Member States rather seem to take advantage of the time factor and benefit from the 59-month duration of the procedure under Article 226 EC. A provision similar to that of Article 88 ECSC would not exclude such behaviour, as legal certainlty would not be definitely obtained prior to a judgment by the Court. And even if this were different, the true deterrent sanction for Member States is the threat of a penalty payment under Article 228 EC. However, this procedure generally takes, between the dispatch of the first letter of formal notice under Article 226 EC and the judgment of the Court under Article 228, on average nine years in environmental matters! Even shortening this period by one or two years would not really improve the delays in transposing EC environmental law.

4 Decentralising environmental dispute settlement

During the preparation of the White Paper on European Governance, a Commission working group examined the different aspects of 'decentralisation: better involvement of national, regional and local actors'.[18] With regard to the question of enforcement, the group stated:

'The Community institutions – Court of Justice and Commission – are increasingly asked to intervene on a daily basis to force the national authorities to discharge their Community legislation obligations correctly. This situation, which is likely to worsen with enlargement, involves a heavy centralised workload for these institutions and a consequent risk of reduced effectiveness'.[19]

---

[17] Since 1992, the Court has delivered judgment in 36 cases where the Member State had not transmitted the necessary measures to transpose EC environmental directives into national law. In a further 32 cases, the transposition was incomplete or incorrect and in 49 cases the transposed EC law was being badly applied.

[18] European Commission, European Governance; preparatory work for the White Paper. Work Area No.3: Improving the exercise of executive responsibilities. Luxembourg 2002, at 133 *et seq.*

[19] European Commission (note 18), at 191.

The working group recommended that a decentralised implementation of
Community law should be considered, in particular by the creation and organisation of specific appeals machinery in secondary legislation, improved legal
training and information, the simplification and consolidation of EC law, legal
assistance with the interpretation of EC law, solutions for reducing the costs
of access to justice, the creation, in all Member States and/or large regions, of
an ombudsman or a complaint body and it mentioned, on several occasions,
the leading role that could be played by the environmental sector. The working
group then continued:

> 'Should regional Community law courts be set up, namely Community courts
> functioning as courts of first instance in the various Member States and/or regions?
> This option would make it possible to have the advantages of decentralisation, but
> without breaking the link between the citizens and the Community institutions. It has
> not been opted for up until now because it raises several difficult questions. Only the
> principle of specialised courts at central level was agreed in Nice'.[20]

These remarks have the double merit of bringing the question of regional
Community law courts into the discussion and of pointing to the fact that
access to the courts is not an issue which should be discussed on its own. In
environmental matters – and this contribution deliberately limits itself to this
issue – the decisive challenge for lawyers is to protect the environment with the
means of law. This means in concrete terms that it is less relevant by whom or
by which institution the environment is protected rather than that the environment is protected at all. This is the reason why questions of nation-State sovereignty, of competence and of the division of responsibilities make so little sense
for the environment which knows no frontiers. In legal terms what matters is
that the numerous international conventions on the protection of the environment, EC regulations and directives, national, regional and local provisions are
effectively applied and ensure the effective protection of the environment. The
question of the body which is responsible for enforcement and of the responsible
court is subordinate to this problem, and where it is placed at the forefront of
the discussion, this is mainly done for reasons of maintenance of power, efforts
to retain influence and to control the process, thus in the end for egotistical
reasons, not so much for reasons of protecting, preserving and improving the
quality of the environment.

The problem of 'European courts in environmental matters' therefore needs
to be enlarged to cover the protection of the environment by European law. As
the basic rule contained in Article 211 EC, which requires the Commission to

---

[20] European Commission (note 18), at 193; the specialised courts at the 'central level' are the above-
mentioned 'judicial panels'.

ensure that EC environmental law is effectively applied, will not be modified, it needs to be examined to what extent monitoring the application of EC environmental law could be decentralised.

Where the transposition of EC environmental legislation into national law is in question, Member States are normally obliged to transmit to the Commission the provisions of national, regional or local law which transpose EC law into national law. Controlling, whether such legislation has been adopted and the possible sending of letters of formal notice or reasoned opinions, could also be delegated to decentralised bodies. However, not much would be gained by such a procedure, as such information would in any case have to be sent to the central Community institution and assessed there, for reasons of monitoring, of environmental policy-making and policy amendment, of integration with other policies, of attributing of financial support under structural funds etc., on the one hand, and for reasons of equal treatment of Member States with regard to delays, transposition requirements etc., on the other.

Similar considerations apply to the second step in the evaluation of national legislation: determining whether national environmental legislation completely and correctly transposes EC environmental legislation into national law. Again, the equal treatment of EC Member States, the uniform interpretation of the different provisions of EC law and the interdependency between the environment and other EC policies and legal provisions rather advocate a continuation of the centralised evaluation of national legislation.

Things may, however, be different as regards the third element, i.e. controlling the effective application of EC environmental law. While it may be a relatively simple matter to adopt legislation, it is another thing to efficiently apply it. Most cases of environmental impairment through land use, destruction of habitats, or the discharge of pollutants also have a clear local dimension. It is for the reason of the omnipresence of environmental impairment that the effective application of environmental law is the most crucial challenge within environmental law. The Commission has no inspectors to examine if and how EC environmental law is applied in practice. Member States were only ready to accept a non-binding recommendation on the setting up of national inspectors in order to control the application of local, regional, national, EC or international environmental provisions. This refusal to have EC environmental inspectors was justified by subsidiarity considerations, although the EC does have inspectors to control the effective application of food and veterinary legislation, competition and fishery legislation, and regional policy and customs legislation, which reveals the ideological nature of the argument.

Anyway, even in the most centralised of the above-mentioned systems, competition policy, the EU has recently decentralised the control mechanism and has the application of EC competition rules applied and monitored by decentralised bodies at the national level.[21] In the environmental sector, the

---

[21] See Regulation 1/2003, OJ 2003, L 1/1.

most important means of informating the Commission of cases of poor application is the vigilance of citizens, local groups, NGOs and, generally, persons who
care for the environment. The tool by which to transmit this information to the
European Commission is the complaint procedure which is at present located
at the European Commission. Other means such as petitions to the European
Parliament, written or oral questions by Parliament or the intergovernmental
IMPEL network play a very subordinate role.

Nothing could prevent Member States from setting up national systems
or centres for the monitoring of (EC) environmental legislation which would
receive complaints concerning the poor application of environmental legal provisions. The advantage of such systems would be that such decentralised centres
would be able to examine and assess the facts of a given compliant as regards
poor application much quicker than the present centralised system. The reasons
for this are first of all the linguistics: it must be expected that in an enlarged
EC a number of documents on a specific case of the poor application of EC law
will have to be translated from a less well known to a more common language.
Examples could be the omission to make environmental impact assessments, to
monitoring a natural habitat or the authorisation of an infrastructure project.

Another reason is the geographical proximity of the complaint monitoring
centre to the case in question which would allow the factual situation to be clarified much quicker. The proximity is also relevant for the better knowledge of
local, regional and national legal provisions which would apply in a given case.
Finally, the question of human resources would probably be less problematic
than at the level of an enlarged EC.

There is certainly also the risk that such centres, which are necessarily set
up by public authorities, are not neutral but take the side of the (local, regional
or national) administration and that they rank economic interests – for instance
farming, regional development, investors – higher than environmental interests.
At present, this phenomenon can occasionally be observed even at the local
courts. I see only one way to prevent such phenomena from regularly occur-
ring: transparency in decision-making, the discussion of decisions in public and
democratic controversies. Overall, however, this risk is not sufficiently strong to
generally object to the establishment of such centres.

As the establishment of such decentralised complaint centres by Member
States would not make Article 211 EC disappear, the role of the Commission
and of its obligations under that provision would have to be clarified. However,
this is more a practical rather than a theoretical problem. Even at present, only
about fifteen percent of all environmental complaints raised with the European
Commission lead to the opening of formal legal proceedings under Article 226
EC, whether this is because the complaint is unjustified, or because the Member
State in question has, upon representations by the Commission, rectified the
situation.

Under these circumstances, one might conceive a system which gives environmental decentralised complaint centres the possibility to instruct and to decide on environmental complaints. The European Commission would normally accept such a decision – which could also consist of a recommendation to the Commission to open formal proceedings under Article 226 EC. A specific clause could provide that in very exceptional cases the Commission would have the right to overturn the decision on a specific complaint, for instance where there has been a gross error in the assessment or a gross omission in considering a specific legal provision of EC law or where there has been a significant deviation from the established application of certain principles under EC environmental law. Furthermore, a clause would be required to the effect that the Commission would have the possibility to examine the complaint itself without waiting for the decision by the national complaint centre, where a decision has not been taken within a specific period of time.

5 Decentralised environmental courts

The question whether there should be decentralised courts to decide on EC environmental law is not easy to answer and certainly goes far beyond monitoring the application of environmental law. Federal courts at State level exist in the United States and although my knowledge of the US judicial system is very limited, it seems that overall, the problems with the co-existence of federal courts and State courts do not seem to be prohibitive. Of course, the European Union is not and will never be an imitation of the United States. In Europe, there will exist, for the foreseeable future, a diversity in legal cultures, in substantive and procedural law and in languages, paired with the absence of a European public opinion, a *communis opinio*, and a rather precise definition of what the 'general interest of the Community' actually is.[22]

It should be remembered that in all Member States, the judiciary – in a broad sense – is normally rather conservative and less prone to the incorporation of EC law into the national/regional legal system; this phenomenon has led the Commission to state that 'the feeling persists that Community rules are 'foreign laws'.[23] If this observation is correct after forty years of applying of EC law by national/regional courts – and I have no doubt that it is correct as far as environmental law is concerned – one might imagine how the establishment of decentralised European Courts of First Instance would be perceived in at least some EC Member States: they would be seen as implants.

---

[22] This expression is used in Articles 213, 257 (2) and 263(3) EC.

[23] Commission, European Governance, COM (2001) 428 of 25.7.2001, at 25.

It is more than likely that the absorption of such courts by the national/
regional legal and judicial systems would create considerable problems. This will
start with the composition of the courts, as for linguistic reasons, the judges, in
the smaller countries in particular, will essentially come from the indigenous
population. Will the judges then be 'our' judges or 'their' judges? A decision
by such courts is likely to be considered as a victory if it accepts the national/
regional approach; it is likely to be seen as 'treason' where local or regional or
national inconsistencies or 'legal arrangements' are thrown aside.

Another considerable problem is that of the competencies of such courts.
As at present about two-thirds of all environmental cases decided by the Court
of Justice are initiated by the European Commission and ten percent of all
complaints which reach the Commission lead to the initiation of formal proceedings, it might be questioned which cases should be submitted to such decentralised courts. Not much could be gained if Article 226 cases were to be handled
by decentralised courts instead of by the Court of Justice. It should be reiterated
that at present not even the Court of First Instance is entitled to decide on such
cases. All in all, it would probably be a step towards the disintegration of the
European Union if Article 226 cases were attributed to decentralised courts, a
move towards renationalisation.

What other environmental cases could then be handled by such a decentralised court? This raises the general question of dispute settlement in environmental issues. Even if, in the aftermath of the Aarhus Convention, access
to the national or European courts will be made easier, one should not have too
many illusions: humans act according to self-interest. And the great majority
of the 600 or so complaints which reach the European Commission every year
and which deal with environmental issues, have been instigated because of
one individual interest or another on the part of the complainant in having the
environmental impairment halted. Only in a minority of cases is this due to real
concern for the protection or preservation of the environment.

It is true that the situation is normally different as regards complaints
from environmental groups which generally do not pursue their own interests.
However, the number of cases which are capable of being submitted to the
courts by such organisations will necessarily be limited, for reasons of the
personal and financial resources of the environmental group, the costs and duration of litigation and other barriers to access to justice.

This sketchy survey reveals that while there might be a case for considering, in the future, the establishment of decentralised environmental complaint
centres, there does not seem to be a case for having decentralised European
courts. I would not exclude the fact that other sectors – trade mark law or
competition, social issues or product-related issues – of EC policy and law may
offer better perspectives for such decentralised European courts. However,
environmental policy cannot really be taken as an argument in favour of such
development.

CHAPTER 7

Enlargement and its Consequences for EU Environmental Law

Gyula Bándi

1 The EU approach to transitional measures

'Agenda 2000' has emphasized that as none of the candidate countries can be expected to comply fully with the *acquis* in the near future, 'in partnership with the Union, realistic national long-term strategies for gradual effective alignment should be drawn up and start being implemented in all the applicant countries before accession'.[1] A recent report by the Polish government on enlargement[2], summarises the situation as follows: 'Transposition of the environmental *acquis* into the national legal order and its implementation are major tasks.' The list of priority tasks features the following:

- Community framework legislation (including access to information and environmental impact assessment);
- measures relating to international conventions to which the Community is a party;
- reduction of global and transboundary pollution;
- nature protection legislation (aimed at safeguarding bio-diversity),
- measures ensuring the functioning of the internal market (e.g. product standards).

Moreover, in line with Article 6 EC, environmental protection requirements should be integrated in other policy areas in order to contribute to sustainable development.

Based on the general principle that transitional measures should be limited in time and scope, the EU has underlined from the very beginning of the nego-tiations that transitional measures will not be granted as regards transposition (as opposed to implementation) and many other aspects, such as framework legislation or new installations, etc.

2 Importing EU environmental law and policy

The authors' introductory remarks clearly illustrate the present situation: none of the accession countries question the need to transpose EU law into the domestic system. The only exceptions concern certain very special national aspects, for instance concerning the list of protected species or the tem-porary derogation in case of requirements which need large-scale investments or major financial efforts.

---

[1]   Agenda 2000: For a stronger and wider Union, COM(97) 2000, Volume I, Communication, at 65.

[2]   At http://europa.eu.int/comm/enlargement/contacts/poland_en.htm, December 2002.

During the past few years I have had the pleasure to participate first of all in the Hungarian approximation process, but also in that of the Czech Republic[3] and currently in the same process in the SEE countries[4], within which I gained most of my experiences in Bosnia and Herzegovina[5]. In that capacity I have been able to obtain an overview of the situation in those countries which will become EU Member States in 2004 and those which may join at a later stage. The question has always remained the same: how to adapt national environmental legislation to its existing European counterpart. Sometimes, the domestic legislation is already at the same level or is indeed even more advanced – such is the case with nature protection legislation in Hungary – but usually the situation is the opposite. It is no wonder that the issue of the consequences of enlargement for EU environmental law has never been raised!

The Sixth Environmental Action Programme[6] in its Article 2 para. 5. summarizes the tasks of accession countries as follows:

'The Programme shall promote the adoption of policies and approaches that contribute to the achievement of sustainable development in the countries which are candidates for accession ("Candidate Countries") building on the transposition and implementation of the acquis.'

The enlargement process should sustain and protect the environmental assets of the Candidate Countries, such as the wealth of biodiversity, and should maintain and strengthen sustainable production and consumption and land-use patterns and environmentally sound transport structures by means of the following:
- integrating environmental protection requirements into Community Programmes including those related to the development of infrastructures;
- promoting the transfer of clean technologies to the Candidate Countries;
- extending dialogue and exchanging experiences with the national and local administrations in the Candidate Countries on sustainable development and the preservation of their environmental assets;
- cooperating with civil society, environmental non-governmental organisations (NGOs) and business in the Candidate Countries, in order to assist in raising public awareness and participation;
- encouraging international financing institutions and the private sector to

---

[3] Phare Disae Project, CR-106: Upgrading and Implementing Legislative Programmes for Approximation of EU Environmental Legislation in the Czech Republic.

[4] REReP 1.3. project – Assistance in Environmental Law Drafting in South Eastern Europe.

[5] EU PHARE Programme Project – Preparation of Environmental Legislation for Bosnia Herzegovina, Programme Number: BH99-03.

[6] Decision 1600/2002, OJ 2002, L 242/1.

support the implementation of and compliance with the environmental acquis in the Candidate Countries and to pay due attention to integrating environmental concerns into the activities of the economic sector.

This is a clear message – do not question the essence of EU environmental legislation! Let me clarify this without addressing the procedural and general institutional aspects of enlargement in general.

From a national point of view we may distinguish at least three groups of CEE (Central and Eastern European) and SEE (South East European) countries:
- the first group, where national environmental legislation was developed more or less at the beginning of the accession process (the Czech Republic, Hungary, Poland, and probably Slovenia);
- the second group, where environmental legislation was not so much developed at the beginning of the accession process, but where approximation resulted in a relatively rapid progress (the Baltic countries, Bulgaria, Croatia, Romania);
- and, finally, the third group, where, due to several reasons such as armed conflict or weak economic development, the process started relatively late, and also the existing legislation, in terms of environmental protection, was somewhat less developed (Albania, the SEE countries).

The possibility of having an effect on EU legislation is of course greater in the case of the first group than in the case of the third group. Below I will try to extend my overview to all the three groups of countries in order to provide a wider time-frame for accession.

A good example of the above distinction – legislation and implementation capacities – may be the Former Yugoslav Republic of Macedonia. A Stabilization and Association Agreement was signed between the EC and FYR Macedonia on 26 March 2001.[7] Article 103 of the Agreement deals with the priorities of cooperation, where environment has also a place. The Stabilization and Association Report[8] provides a general framework for better understanding:

'4.3.3. Environment: *Following the first National Environmental Action Plan (NEAP), covering the period 1996-2000, a second Plan is now being developed. This takes into account the country's efforts to come closer to EU policies, covering the period of implementation of the SAA. However, a comprehensive medium to long-term strategy is still missing. Major efforts will be needed to progressively approximate*

---

[7] Interinstitutional File: 2001/0049 (ACV).

[8] Commission Staff Working Paper of the Commission of the European Communities on Stabilization, SEC (2002) 342 and Association Report of the Former Yugoslav Republic of Macedonia, COM(2002) 163.

the country's legislative system with the Community environmental acquis. The task is hindered by lack of resources in the environmental authorities.'

While the legislative process is progessing at a relatively rapid pace – every year a series of new laws or amendments to existing laws are being adopted – capacity building is still a problem. The Ministry for the Environment was established in 2000, along with the Agency of the Environment, Spatial Information System and the State Environment Inspectorate. The staffing is still meagre, the role of local governments has not yet been clarified, the monitoring capacity still requires radical improvements, etc.

In Hungary similar problems exist:[9]

'Despite obvious progress, the legal and institutional framework of sustainable development is still weak. ... With the problems of the transition process, attention of the policy-makers, the legislature and the central and local government authorities was constantly drawn to principal issues of democratisation, the economic and social issues, i.e., primarily the requirements of legal and institutional framework of the market economy at the expense of the much more comprehensive and longer-term concept of sustainable development and its implications on health care, education, environment protection, economic development, etc. Problems related to unemployment, income disparities, poverty, unsustainable use of natural resources, rural development were addressed on a rather ad hoc basis, at least from the perspectives of objectives of 'true' sustainable development.'

Furthermore, we should not forget that the requirements under EU environmental legislation may have a great advantage for the future of environmental policy, legislation and implementation. The reason for this is very simple and very well presented in the Hungarian report mentioned above. There are several other objectives at the national level which can overrule the environmental objectives. Obligations under EU law can make a difference in guaranteeing the environmental objectives. [10]

Thus the main problem which is inherent in the accession countries today is how to keep up with European requirements. However, a major task for the EU,

---

[9] Hungary: Basic features and indicators of social, environmental and economic changes and planning for sustainability. National information to the World Summit on Sustainable Development, Johannesburg, 2002, at 21-22.

[10] See also, with respect to Croatia, the Country Strategy Paper on of the major objectives of the 2002-2004 Multi-annual Indicative Program: 'To contribute to the process of alignment of environmental legislation with the acquis;...'. EC External Relations Directorate General, Directorate Western Balkans, CARDS Assistance Programme – Croatia, 2002-2006. Annex 1. Multi-annual Indicative Programme, 2002-2004.

looking at the several difficulties regarding implementation and enforcement, is to develop a structure of permanent monitoring, even during the pre-accession period. If these difficulties cannot be overcome, national environmental measures are not going to be effective. EU environmental legislation will be the strict minimum for all would-be members.

3   A need for change at the EU level?

The next question is whether there is a need to change existing guiding principles, regulatory methods and instruments *within* EU environmental law, or is it necessary to add new provisions to the already existing system? In other words: are there any aspects of national environmental law and policy which can be 'imported' by the EU? This is even more important today, in view of the European Convention as a decisive factor for future developments.

The current national policies prove that all accession countries are willing to follow existing patterns of European environmental legislation. The already available principles and methodology are sufficiently flexible to cover the different national situations. The history of EU enlargement might have taught us that the need for possible changes is stronger where the new members have a more advanced environmental legal system. But even in that case the general EU structures could survive.

Some principles, however, may have a different emphasis. For example, in the case of mass privatisation, which is still an ongoing process in the CEE and SEE countries, and also in the case of decisions on new investments, there is a major threat that environmental interest will be pushed to the background and that long-lasting environmental values will be neglected. This would mean a need to revitalize existing principles, like the precautionary principle and the prevention principle. Also the polluter pays principle may have a special meaning, taking into consideration the enduring role of state property within certain national economies. A clear understanding of the polluter pays principle will lead to regulations on state liability or at least a responsibility to remedy a situation in those cases where the successor cannot be held liable.

Let us take a look at the method of self-regulation, that is voluntary agreements as forthcoming methods in accession countries. It would apparently be easier to use such methods in order to fill the gaps which are the result of inefficient enforcement capacities. The picture seems to be clear: self-regulation and self-implementation on the part of potential polluters may replace, to a certain extent, the role of direct intervention by the authorities.[11] However, this is far from reality in the accession countries, as voluntary measures, such as agree-

---

[11] Cf. the concept of 'working with the market' in the 6th Environmental Action Programme.

ments, may only be effective if an efficient environmental enforcement capacity is available. There has to be an enforcement capacity which is capable of managing the agreement procedure, monitoring the implementation and reacting to any defects. Thus the possible relief, if any, is only available to countries with an already existing and well-developed public administration.

Also actually using new regulatory methods and techniques may be problematic. The history of environmental legislation demonstrates that states usually start by using traditional environmental instruments, like command-and-control measures. Based on the experiences gained, a solid basis for using new instruments can be established. In other words, cooperation skills and the practice of control have to be learned.

The same is true for such regulatory methods as the use of 'technology requirements' – most importantly BAT – which actually means the individualisation of environmental requirements, together with the need to be aware of technology development tendencies, being able to find the proper balance between the best and environmentally necessary techniques, the costs of investment and the possible environmental damage, the social and environmental impact, etc.

On the other hand, existing European principles and regulatory methods may help a great deal in developing an environmental legal system in accession countries. Even today in most of these countries more or less all the principles are laid down in legislative acts. And in many countries the right to a sound environment is a constitutional right. It can be expected that, together with the transposition of substantive European environmental standards, the different instruments will be transposed as well.

4 Changing the Treaty provisions?

Is there a need to change the environmental provisions of Treaty due to the enlargement process?

Article 95 para. 3 EC states:

'The Commission, in its proposals envisaged in paragraph 1 concerning health, safety, environmental protection and consumer protection, will take as a base a high level of protection, taking account in particular of any new development based on scientific facts. Within their respective powers, the European Parliament and the Council will also seek to achieve this objective.'

From the point of view of accession countries, nothing new should be added, but it would be useful to implement these principles in practice. There is every opportunity that the strategic environmental assessment directive[12] may provide some substance in this respect.

Article 95 paras. 4-6 provide the possibility for Member States to derogate from harmonised European standards:

'4. If, after the adoption by the Council or by the Commission of a harmonisation measure, a Member State deems it necessary to maintain national provisions on grounds of major needs referred to in Article 30, or relating to the protection of the environment or the working environment, it shall notify the Commission of these provisions as well as the grounds for maintaining them.

5. Moreover, without prejudice to paragraph 4, if, after the adoption by the Council or by the Commission of a harmonisation measure, a Member State deems it necessary to introduce national provisions based on new scientific evidence relating to the protection of the environment or the working environment on grounds of a problem specific to that Member State arising after the adoption of the harmonisation measure, it shall notify the Commission of the envisaged provisions as well as the grounds for introducing them.

6. The Commission shall, within six months of the notifications as referred to in paragraphs 4 and 5, approve or reject the national provisions involved after having verified whether or not they are a means of arbitrary discrimination or a disguised restriction on trade between Member States and whether or not they shall constitute an obstacle to the functioning of the internal market.
In the absence of a decision by the Commission within this period the national provisions referred to in paragraphs 4 and 5 shall be deemed to have been approved.'

With respect to maintaining of an already existing national provision, there is not too much to say. In the light of Article 95 para. 6, we might even say that the possibility of maintaining more stringent national measures is a part of the negotiating process. Thus the same problem may only emerge after accession. But why should the new Member States be given a special privilege not to use this clause? The same can be said with respect to para. 5. Generally speaking, there may not be too many cases of stricter national measures. In Hungary, for example, some nature conservation measures may be considered to be stricter, or at least different, but these may not be considered to have too much of an impact on the functioning of the internal market, so the problem does not arise. Our conclusion is that, from practical reasons, there is no need to add to or amend these provisions.

---

[12] Directive 2001/42 on the assessment of the effects of certain plans and programmes on the environment, OJ 2001, L 197/30.

Article 174, para. 1 EC lists the objectives of European environmental policy. The only matter which may be raised here as a possible additional element to be listed is a reference to future generations. Such a reference appears in a number of national constitutions or framework acts. The mere reference in Article 174 (1) EC to human health is a restriction as compared with those national constitutional developments.

The Hungarian Environmental Act states in its preamble:[13]

'Considering the fact that the natural heritage and environmental values are part of the national wealth, their preservation and conservation and the improvement of their quality are primary conditions from the aspect of the health and quality of life of the biosphere, and of humans in particular; without them, no harmony between human activities and nature can be maintained, neglecting them would pose a hazard to the health of present generations, the existence of future generations and the survival of a number of species, therefore, Parliament, in agreement with the Constitution, creates the following Act:...'

Article 74 of the Polish Constitution reads:[14]

'1. Public authorities shall pursue policies ensuring the ecological security of current and future generations.'

Thus, a reference in the EC Treaty to the protection of future generations as part of the objectives of Community environmental policy might be a useful notion to pursue.

Article 174, para. 2 EC acknowledges the principles upon which European environmental policy is based:

'Community policy on the environment shall aim at a high level of protection taking into account the diversity of situations in the various regions of the Community. It shall be based on the precautionary principle and on the principles that preventive action should be taken, that environmental damage should as a priority be rectified at source and that the polluter should pay'.

---

[13] Act LIII of 1995 on the general provisions of environmental protection.

[14] As adopted by the National Assembly on 2 April 1997.

These environmental principles are all mentioned in the different environmental laws of the accession countries. The Model Act of the Council of Europe drafted for CEE countries[15] lists the following principles:
- precautionary principle;
- substitution;
- maintenance of biodiversity;
- non-degradation of natural resources;
- polluter pays;
- right of the public to information and participation;
- cooperation.

Also sustainable development may either be taken as an objective or as a principle.

Principle 10 of the Rio Declaration on Environment and Development can be regarded as the basic provision in the field of public participation:

'Environmental issues are best handled with the participation of all concerned citizens, at the relevant level. At national level, each individual shall have appropriate access to information concerning the environment that is held by public authorities, including information on hazardous materials and activities in their communities, and the opportunity to participate in decision-making processes. States shall facilitate and encourage public awareness and participation by making information widely available. Effective access to judicial and administrative proceedings, including redress and remedy, shall be provided.'

The EC itself is very close to ratifying of the Convention on Access to Information, Public Participation in Decision-Making and Access to Justice in Environmental Matters, the so-called *Aarhus Convention*, and to implementing it fully within the Community legal order.[16] If we look at the list of principles, taking into consideration their role in the accession countries (and here I also mean those countries which are in the second or third group of would-be members), we may propose the adoption of two additional principles and to be added to the list in Article 174 (2) EC: public participation and cooperation. Both have their

---

[15] See http://www.eel.nl/legislation/COE-Model_Act_1994.htm. This document was prepared in 1994 by a group of independent experts within the framework of the co-operation programme between the Council of Europe and the Central and Eastern European countries. It is designed as a model for a revision of existing legislation or the adoption of new legislation.

[16] See the proposal for a Council Decision on the signature by the European Community of the UN/ECE Convention on access to information, public participation and access to justice in environmental matters; COM (1998) 344 final.

firm basis in the EU legal system, but what is much more important, both may have a major effect in the development of domestic environmental policy and legislation.

The principle of cooperation corresponds with the obligation of the state to enhance public participation. Cooperation shall be the guiding principle in the relationship between the state, users of environmental resources and the public at large. Another aspect of cooperation is the problem of what is known as 'shared responsibility'. The EC's Fifth Environmental Action Programme[17] states:

'Since the objectives and targets put forward in the Programme and the ultimate goal of sustainable development can only be achieved by concerted action on the part of all the relevant actors working together in partnership, the Programme combines the principle of subsidiarity with the wider concept of shared responsibility. This latter concept involves not so much a choice of action at one level to the exclusion of others but, rather, a mixing of actors and instruments at the appropriate levels, without any calling into question of the division of competencies between the Community, the Member States, regional and local authorities. For any one target or problem, the emphasis (actors and instruments) could lie with the Community/national/regional government level and for another with the regional/local/sectoral level or at the level of enterprises/general public/consumers.'

As the obligation to protect the environment is a general obligation and the advantages of a better environmental quality can be felt by everyone, cooperation is in everyone's interest. Agreements pertaining to the regulation of standards or compliance schedules are sometimes more effective than imposing direct obligations. Of course, cooperation faces problems as well, like the greater discretionary authority given to public authorities. Both the Communication from the Commission on Environmental Agreements and the Sixth Environmental Action Programme cover this aspect. [18]

Both principles have a clear message for the enlargement process, that is to involve stakeholders in a broader way than is common in most of the accession countries.

---

[17] OJ 1993, C 138/1. The citation can be found in chapter 8.

[18] Communication from the Commission on Environmental Agreements; COM (96) 561. Cf. also Article 3, para. 5 of the Sixth Environmental Action Programme: 'Improving collaboration and partnership with enterprises and their representative bodies and involving the social partners, consumers and their organisations, as appropriate, with a view to improving the environmental performance of enterprises and aiming at sustainable production patterns. This requires: [...] encouraging voluntary commitments or agreements to achieve clear environmental objectives, including setting out procedures in the event of non-compliance'.

Article 174 para. 3 EC lists the other elements that the Community shall take into account in developing environmental policies. One aspect mentioned is 'environmental conditions in the various regions of the Community'. Regionalism and the problem of diversity in the regions is addressed here. While preserving the essence of that concept, the term 'region' needs to be further elaborated. But then again, it would not be wise to think of CEE or SEE countries as regions in their own right.

Article 175 EC covers the decision-making procedure. I will not examine this issue in detail. The only concern for accession countries might be the need for unanimous voting in issues like town and country planning and land use. This decision-making procedure, in particular with respect to problem areas like town and country planning and land use, may not serve the interest of protecting the environment as this leads to limiting the decision-making capacity. Qualified majority voting may better serve the interests of the environment in accession countries. Otherwise it would be increasingly difficult to reach an agreement on new environmental policies.

5   Introducing a right on environmental protection

Finally, it is worth looking at the existence, or indeed the non-existence, of a right to a environmental protection. Following the 1972 Stockholm Declaration, the Rio Declaration stated in principle no. 1:

'Human beings are at the centre for sustainable development. They are entitled to a healthy and productive life in harmony with nature.'

This prompted Kiss and Shelton[19] to state that:

'Since Stockholm a growing number of international texts have included references to environmental rights or a right to an environment of a certain – or uncertain – quality. [...]Although the 1950 European Convention on Human Rights does not contain a right to environment, case law of the European Commission and Court of Human Rights indicates that environmental deterioration can lead to violations of human rights that are recognized by the convention, including the right to privacy and family life, and the right to property.'

During the past years the importance of such a right has been constantly increasing. In the field of international conventions we may refer to the already

---

[19] Kiss and Shelton (1993), at 43.

mentioned Aarhus Convention. The concept of such a right is mentioned in the preamble and as an 'objective' of the convention. The preamble reads as follows:

'Recognizing also that every person has the right to live in an environment adequate to his or her health and well-being [...]'.

This is repeated in the convention's objective in Article 1:

'In order to contribute to the protection of the right of every person of present and future generations to live in an environment adequate to his or her health and well-being, each Party shall guarantee the rights of access to information, public participation in decision-making, and access to justice in environmental matters in accordance with the provisions of this Convention.'

Here the right to environment is extended to present and future generations.

The importance of environmental rights is also clearly demonstrated in recent judgements of the European Court of Human Rights.[20]

The right to environment as a concept in itself is extremely important, as it implies a right and an obligation at the same time. First of all, the obligation is addressed to the state. So it is the primary obligation for the state to implement the guaranteed environmental rights. Of course, not only the state but other entities as well are obliged to consider human or citizen's rights to environmental protection. In that way the right to sound environment may even be used as a basis for legal action. The already mentioned model draft law of the Council of Europe reads in full:

'Everyone has a right to an ecologically stable and healthy environment. Such a right can be exercised not only in respect of any normative or administrative acts by the public authorities but also in respect of the actions of private persons which are likely to have a significant impact on the environment.'

Among the various national constitutional provisions, I recall an example from Hungary. The first case I want to mention is decision no. 28/1994.(V.20.) of the Hungarian Constitutional Court. In its judgment the court interpreted the constitutional right to environmental protection. Article 18 of the Hungarian Constitution declares that the state recognizes and enforces the right of everyone to a healthy environment. Article 70/D of the Constitution connects this to the right to health, and it also requires a high level of protection.

The case in question concerned the constitutionality of a provision which provided the possibility for the privatisation of nature protection areas. The

---

[20] Cf. on this aspect the contribution by Ermacora in this volume.

major argument used by the Constitutional Court was derived from the concept of environmental rights. According to the Court the level of protection in the field of environmental and nature conservation should not be questioned, only in cases where there is a question of the implementation of other constitutional values or basic rights can be an issue. In other words, the Constitutional Court required a balancing of interests at the same level. The judgment will certainly have a lasting significance on future Hungarian environmental legislation.

The judgment states that the right to a healthy environment constitutes an obligation for the state to establish and maintain a specific institutional system to protect this right. This legal and institutional framework is necessary for the implementation of environmental rights. A mere statement is far from sufficient.

The judgement also stresses that the level of protection is not at the discretion of the state as this protection constitutes the foundations of human life and that harm to the environment is usually irreparable. The need for a certain level of protection leads to a strict regime of environmental security. Thus the state is free to choose from, among the various means and methods of protection, but has no freedom in allowing any form of or even the risk of degradation.

One paragraph of the decision explains that in the field of environmental protection prevention has priority over sanctions. Prevention as a requirement can only be effective if a legal framework has already been established for such protection. The lack of preventive measures was one reason for the judgment. As was already mentioned, private ownership of nature conservation areas is not unconstitutional in itself, but combined with a lack of the necessary legal and institutional safeguards it may threaten nature conservation. In such a situation sanctions and prohibitions are not enough. A system of preventive measures has to be established.

If we look at other CEE or SEE countries, then we come to the same conclusion:

a) The right to environmental protection is reflected in the new Albanian Constitution as the state is to provide 'for a healthy and ecologically suitable environment for present and future generations' and 'for the rational utilization of forests, water resources, pastures, based on the principle of sustainable development'. The same right is at the centre of the Constitutional right of each individual 'to be informed of the state of the environment and its protection.' – as it reads in the Albanian report to Johannesburg[21].

---

[21] Republic of Albania Ministry of Environment: National Assessment Report for the World Summit on Sustainable Development Johannesburg, 26 August – 4 September 2002 -Tirana, July 2002; http://www.johannesburgsummit.org/html/prep_process/national_reports/albania_natl_assess_1208.pdf.

b) The Constitution of Bosnia and Herzegovina in its Article III (Responsibilities of and Relations between the Institutions of Bosnia and Herzegovina and the Entities) declares that:

'2. Responsibilities of the Entities ... c. The Entities shall provide a safe and secure environment for all persons in their respective jurisdictions, by maintaining civilian law enforcement agencies operating in accordance with internationally recognized standards and with respect for the internationally recognized human rights and fundamental freedoms referred to in Article II above, and by taking such other measures as appropriate.'

c) The 1992 Constitution of the Federal Republic of Yugoslavia acknowledges the right to a healthy environment. In its Article 52 it states as follows:

'Man shall be entitled to a healthy environment and timely information about its condition. It is everyone's duty to protect the human environment and make use of it in a rational manner. The state shall be charged with maintaining a healthy human environment and to this end shall prescribe the conditions and manner of the performance of economic and other activities.'

d) The Polish Constitution[22] has several references to this right: Article 74 – 1. Public authorities shall pursue policies ensuring the ecological security of current and future generations. 2. Protection of the environment shall be the duty of public authorities. 3. Everyone shall have the right to be informed of the quality of the environment and its protection. 4. Public authorities shall support the activities of citizens to protect and improve the quality of the environment. Article 86 – Everyone shall care for the quality of the environment and shall be held responsible for causing its degradation. The principles of such responsibility shall be specified by statute.

The Charter of Fundamental Rights of the European Union[23] says in the Preamble:

'Conscious of its spiritual and moral heritage, the Union is founded on the indivisible, universal values of human dignity, freedom, equality and solidarity; it is based on the principles of democracy and the rule of law. It places the individual at the heart of its activities, by establishing the citizenship of the Union and by creating an area of freedom, security and justice. The Union contributes to the preservation and to the development of these common values while respecting the diversity of

---

[22] As adopted by the National Assembly on 2nd April 1997.

[23] Adopted by the European Parliament, the Council and the Commission on December 7, 2000.

the cultures and traditions of the peoples of Europe as well as the national identities
of the Member States and the organisation of their public authorities at national,
regional and local levels; it seeks to promote balanced and sustainable development
and ensures free movement of persons, goods, services and capital, and the freedom of
establishment. To this end, it is necessary to strengthen the protection of fundamental
rights in the light of changes in society, social progress and scientific and technological
developments by making those rights more visible in a Charter.'

In Article 37 of the Charter it is stated:

'A high level of environmental protection and the improvement of the quality
of the environment must be integrated into the polices of the Union and ensured in
accordance with the principle of sustainable development.'

On the one hand, it is of great value that environmental protection is mentioned
within a human rights charter, but, on the other, this is far from being satisfac-
tory. These words do not elaborate upon what has already been reflected in the
Treaty provisions. And it is rather modest compared to any of constitutions of
the CEE or SEE discussed above. The present formulation of the Charter does
not reflect the importance of environmental protection as a third generation
human right and it is not formulated either as a human right, nor as an obligation towards the Member States or towards the EU itself. Enlargement should
not have the result that the EU takes a backward step from an already generally
accepted national constitutional right to environmental protection.

Thus the 'message from enlargement countries' may be summarised as
follows:
- consider the right to environmental protection to be a genuine right and
  not a 'solidarity' issue;
- use the wording 'right to environmental protection' and combine it with a
  reference to present and future generations;
- refer to the obligation of the EU and the Member States to protect this
  right;
- refer to the obligation of all interested parties, stakeholders, and the people
  to protect this right.

Resolution of the Avosetta Conference 11 & 12 October, 2002, Amsterdam

Preamble

The Avosetta Group is a small informal group of lawyers whose main purpose is to further the development of environmental law in the European Union and its Member States. *Avosetta* is the Latin name of a rare bird which resulted in the European Court of Justice establishing far-reaching principles of European nature protection law in the *German Leybucht* case. The group held its inaugural meeting at Bremen University in January 2001.

Those participating in Avosetta are invited due to the recognition of their outstanding distinction in European environmental law, and they take part in a personal and independent capacity. Nevertheless, Avosetta discussions aim to reflect a comprehensive cross-section of legal cultures within Europe, and will generally include up to two participants from each Member and accession States.

At its meeting on October 11 and 12, 2002, held in Amsterdam it adopted a resolution on *The European Convention and the Future of European Environmental Law*. In view of the draft 'Constitutional Treaty' presented by the Praesidium of the Convention on October 28, 2002, the final text of the Avosetta Conference was approved on November 2, 2002.

1. The integration principle of Article 6 EC should be maintained in the new Constitutional Treaty under Title III: 'Union Competences and Actions'.

2. The objectives and principles in the current treaties (Article 2 EU; Articles 2, 6, 174 EC) on environmental protection and sustainable development do not need any major changes, but should be maintained in the new Constitutional Treaty. The following amendments would however be advisable:
   (a) to include in Article 174 (1) fourth indent a reference to possible 'unilateral' measures. The text of Article 174 (1) fourth indent will then read as follows: 'promoting measures at international level to deal with regional or worldwide environmental problems. Such measures may include unilateral ones, without prejudice to other international obligations'.
   (b) to include in Article 174 (2) the principle of 'sustainable development'.
   (c) to include in Article 174 (2) the principle of 'inter-generational equity'. The text of Article 174 (2, second sentence) should then read as follows: 'It shall be based on the principle of sustainable development, the principle of inter-generational equity, the precautionary principle and on the principles that preventive action should be taken, that environmental damage should as a priority be rectified at source and that the polluter should pay.'

3. All decisions on environmental affairs (Articles 174-176 EC) should be taken by co-decision. We suggest that Article 175 (2) EC should be deleted.

(1) As for provisions of a fiscal nature, taxes in general (including the 'greening' of general taxes) are in any event to be founded on Articles 90 to 93. Article 175 can only be the basis for special environmental charges which are not taxes in the proper understanding of the term, such as, for example, a charge on aircraft emissions, on the discharge of waste water, etc. The same is true for the selling of emission rights. As these measures are environmental protection instruments complementing or replacing more traditional 'direct and supervise' measures, there is no reason why they should be decided by special procedures.

(2) As for measures concerning town and country planning, land use and the management of water resources, these should indeed remain the primary competence of the Member States. This can however best be secured if they are not mentioned at all as a Community competence. The directives given by Article 175 paragraph 1 EC provide sufficient guidance not to allow intrusion into these competences if they are not specially required by environmental concerns.

(3) As for energy policy measures 'significantly affecting a Member States' choice' will in most cases anyway be based on Article 155 and/or Article 86. Should there be specific environmental goals to be attained in the energy policy field these measures do not significantly differ from other environmental protection measures. Therefore they should be decided according to the same procedures.

4. The group has discussed whether the participation of environmental associations should be strengthened along the lines provided for management and labour according to Article 138 and 139 EC. It is of the opinion, however, that the legislative procedure and the rules on access to information provide sufficient opportunities for public participation. Nevertheless, and in order to ensure effective and balanced representation of environmental interests in the making of secondary legislation and executive rules, Article 174 should be amended by a paragraph 3a which could read as follows: 'Before submitting proposals in the environmental policy field, the Commission shall consult environmental protection associations ensuring balanced participation'.

Dialogue and consultation between NGOs and the Commission have to be seen within the framework of the decision-making procedures of Article 175 EC. In other words: dialogue and consultation to enhance the quality of the Commission's right of initiative. Of course this is not only relevant to environmental policy making, but in general one can say that timely consultations with all the stakeholders concerned could improve the quality of the Commission's proposals (Aarhus!). There are other means to enhance a European-wide public debate on environmental affairs. The Commission could organise – in the pre-proposal stage – things like public hearings, and society-wide-discussion. Not on all, but on the important issues (Water Framework Directive; EIA, Habitats Directive and so on).

5. The following provision should be inserted in the new Constitutional Treaty: 'Subject to imperative reasons of overriding public interest, significantly impairing the environment or human health shall be prohibited'. We suggest that this provision should be part of the environment paragraph in the new Constitutional Treaty (Part II, A3, V).

    The proposed amendment to the Treaty is inspired by the case law on the EC Treaty's Articles 28-30 and has four functions. First, the intention is to ensure that environmental interests/protection in the balance of interests has at least the same priority as free trade. Second, the intention is to give environmental protection direct effect, requiring EU institutions as well as Member States and their citizens not to take decisions or undertake activities which significantly impair the environment or human health, unless such impairment can be reasoned by overriding public interest. Third, the scope is limited to 'significant impairment' to ensure, that the courts focus on substantial issues, which leave some discretion for minor impairment. Fourth, when the impairing source (the polluter, the project, the use of natural resources and so on) or the effected part of the environment are covered by EC legislation, it is the EC legislation which defines what is acceptable and, thereby, what is significant, in the same way as exhaustive harmonization pre-empts Member States from recalling the EC Treaty's Article 30. The Avosetta Group find that the proposed amendment establishes a fair and reasonable balance between environmental protection and the importance of leaving discretion for policy-makers.

6. The Charter of Fundamental Rights of the European Union should be integrated in the Treaty. Instead of Article 37 (a provision similar to the Integration Principle of Article 6 EC) of the Charter the following text should be added:

    'Everyone has the right to a clean natural environment. This right is subject to reasons of overriding public interest. It includes the right to participation in decision making, the right of access to the courts and the right to information in environmental matters. A high level of environmental protection and the improvement of the quality of the environment must be integrated into the policies of the Union and ensured in accordance with the principle of sustainable development'.

Both the European Court of Human Rights and the European Court of Justice recognize a right, or certain elements of such a right, of individuals to a clean environment. In various instances the courts have developed this case law in spite of the absence of legal provisions explicitly attributing rights in environmental matters to individuals. The basis for the respective findings of the ECHR are both the right to life and the right to respect for private and family life as set out in the Convention for the Protection of Human Rights and Fundamental Freedoms. The recognition of a violation of the said human right through the impairment of the environment is, however, limited to cases of the immediate impact of environmental pollution, such as noise, smells and emissions, on individuals living in the vicinity of the respective polluter.

Most European constitutions expressly recognise a right to a clean environment in one form or another (Article 66 of the Portuguese Constitution, Article 45 of the Spanish Constitution, Article 24.1 of the Greek Constitution, Article 21 of the Dutch Constitution, Article 23 of the Belgian Constitution, Articles 2 and 73-80 of the Swiss Constitution, Article 20a of the German Constitution, Article 14A of the Finnish Constitution, Article 110B of the Norwegian Constitution). Even in those cases where the Constitution does not expressly recognise this right, it might be stipulated in framework laws (for example Article L-110-2 of the French Environmental Code.).
All these constitutional and legal provisions give rise to both rights and obligations – rights to the extent that most of these Constitutional provisions recognise, either explicitly or implicitly, the right of citizens to be able to live in a healthy, balanced or protected environment. As we shall see below, procedural rights follow from this fundamental constitutional right, particularly as regards information, participation and access to justice.
Enshrining a proper right to a clean natural environment would allow individuals to take action against the impairment of environmental media, which would in many cases only indirectly, over a certain distance or after a certain time, lead to the actual prejudice of their well-being. Such preventive action against the impairment of the environment conforms with the basic principles of EC environmental law set out in Article 174 EC and according to which precautionary and preventive action should be taken, environmental damage should as a priority be rectified at source and the polluter should pay. The cited environmental directing principles may strengthen constitutional provisions that recognise environmental protection by setting out markers for action by public authorities. In other words, the recognition of a constitutional right to environment only has meaning if it is informed by principles whose function is, precisely, to guide the public authorities in taking action intended to protect the environment more effectively.

The right to a clean environment is not absolute. Public, including economic interests might limit the breadth of the right to a clean environment. Such interests need, however, to be of overriding importance for the public. For other cases, the proposed formulation ensures that – when balancing varying interests – the interest of environmental protection enjoys at least the same importance as economic rights, such as the right to property or the free movement of goods.

7. The right to participation in decision making, the right of access to the courts and the right to information in environmental matters are an integral part of the right to a clean environment. The explicit mentioning of these rights pays tribute to the UN/ECE Convention on Access to Information, Public Participation in Decision-Making and Access to Justice in Environmental Matters (Aarhus Convention), which needs to be implemented into Community law.

8. Article 230 para. 4 EC should be redrafted in order to enhance the possibilities of NGOs and other parties concerned to bring an action before the ECJ for annulment of measures affecting the environment. We suggest either deleting the words 'and individual' or replacing the term 'individual' with 'significant' in the said paragraph.

    In the light of the recent ECJ judgment of July 25, 2002, in Case C-50/00 P *UPA*, the conclusion must be that legal protection against measures of the EU institutions affecting the environment remains unsatisfactorily. The ECJ itself concluded that the only way to change the current situation is to change the EC Treaty (Article 230). We suggest that this invitation by the ECJ should be followed.

9. A system of division of powers between the EU institutions and the Member States on the basis of a so-called *Kompetenz-Katalog* should be avoided. A further strengthening of the subsidiarity-principle could also impair the development of European environmental law and is therefore also to be rejected.

10. Member States must have the right to maintain and take more stringent environmental measures than the European ones. Articles 176 and 95 4-6 EC must be formulated in a more parallel way. In doing so, the following guidelines should be respected:
    • The distinction between existing and newly introduced measures should be abolished;
    • The Member State has to prove – when the more stringent standards affect

the functioning of the Internal Market, that the measures meet the proportionality principle;
• A review procedure by the Community should be maintained.

11. On the enforcement of European law in general and environmental law in particular we suggest amending the Treaty infringement procedure (Article 226 EC) so that it is more similar to the procedure in the ECSC Treaty (Article 88 ECSC; not longer in force).

The Avosetta Group, Amsterdam November 5, 2002.

List of participants at the Amsterdam Conference:

1. Prof. Dr. Gyula Bándi, Pàzmány Péter Catholic University
2. Prof. Dr. Astrid Epiney, Institut für Europarecht, Universität Freiburg
3. Dr. Florian Ermacora, Law Firm of Schönherr Rechtsanwälte OEG
4. Dr. Barbara Iwanska , Department of Environmental Protection Law, Jagiellonian University
5. Prof. Dr. Jan H. Jans, European Law Institute, University of Amsterdam
6. Prof. Dr. Jerzy Jendroska, Centrum Prawa Ekologicznego, Wroclaw
7. Prof. Richard Macrory, Faculty of Laws, University College London
8. Prof. Angel-Manuel Moreno, Universidad Carlos III de Madrid
9. Prof. Dr. Peter Pagh, Københavns Universitet
10. Prof. Dr. Glykeria Sioutis, University of Athens
11. Prof. Dr. Gerd Winter, Forschungsstelle für Europaeisches Umweltrecht, University of Bremen
12. Prof. Dr. Hanna G. Sevenster, University of Amsterdam
13. J. Janssen, LL.M., University of Amsterdam
14. Prof. Dr. Nicolas de Sadeleer, Centre d'étude du droit de l'environnement, l'Université de Saint-Louis à Bruxelles
15. Dr. M. Montini (University of Siena)

Observer

1. Prof. Dr. Ludwig Krämer, European Commission, DG Environment

Bibliography

ALEXY (1986)

R. Alexy, *Theorie der Grundrechte* (Frankfurt 1986).

BIEBER (2001)

R. Bieber, 'Abwegige und zielführende Vorschläge: zur Kompetenzabgrenzung der Europäischen Union', (2001) *Integration*, 308 *et seq.*

BOGDANDY & BAST (2001)

A. Bogdandy & J. Bast, 'Die vertikale Kompetenzordnung der EU. Rechtsdogmatischer Bestand und verfassungspolitische Reformperspektiven', (2001) *EuGRZ*, 441 *et seq.*

BUNGENBERG (2000)

M. Bungenberg, 'Dynamische Integration, Art. 308 und die Forderung nach einem Kompetenzkatalog', (2000) *EuR*, 879 *et seq.*

CALLIESS (2002)

C. Calliess, in: Calliess/Ruffert (Hrsg.), *Kommentar zu EU-Vertrag und EG-Vertrag* [Art. 175] (Baden-Baden 2002).

CAMERON (1994)

J. Cameron, P. Demaret and D. Geradin (eds.), *Trade and Environment: the Search for a Balance* (London 1994).

CHALMERS (1998)

D. Chalmers, 'External Relations and the periphery of EU environmental law', in F. Weiss, E. Denters, P. De Waart, *International Law with a Human Face* (The Hague 1998).

DASHWOOD (1998)

A. Dashwood, 'Implied External Competence of the EC', in M. Koskenniemi, *International Law Aspects of the European Union* (The Hague 1998), 113 *et seq.*

DASHWOOD & HILLION (2000)

A. Dashwood & C. Hillion, *The General Law of EC External Relations* (London 2000).

DASHWOOD & HELISKOSKI (2000)

A. Dashwood & J. Heliskoski, 'The Classic Authorities Revisited', in A. Dashwood & C. Hillion, *The General Law of EC External Relations* (London 2000), 3 *et seq.*

DASHWOOD (2000A)

A. Dashwood, 'The Attribution of External Relations Competence', in A. Dashwood & C. Hillion, *The General Law of EC External Relations* (London 2000), 115 *et seq.*

DE SADELEER (2000)

N. de Sadeleer, 'Les fondements de l'action communautaire en matière d'environnement', in: L. le Hardy de Beaulieu (éd.), *L' Europe et ses citoyens*, (Bruxelles, Bern, Berlin, Frankfurt/M., New York, Oxford, Wien 2000).

DE SADELEER (2002)

N. de Sadeleer, *Environmental principles. From political slogans to legal rules* (Oxford 2002).

DESGAGNÉ (1995)

R. Desgagné, 'Integrating environmental values into the ECHR' (1995) *AJIL* 263 *et seq.*

DWORKIN (1977)

R. Dworkin, *Taking rights seriously* (Cambridge 1977).

EPINEY (1995)

A. Epiney, *Umgekehrte Diskriminierungen* (Köln 1995).

EPINEY (1997)

A. Epiney, *Umweltrecht in der EU* (München 1997).

EPINEY (1999)

A. Epiney, 'Gemeinschaftsrecht und Verbandsklage', *NVwZ* 1999, 485.

EPINEY & SOLLBERGER (2001)

A. Epiney & K. Sollberger, *Zugang zu Gerichten und gerichtliche Kontrolle im Umweltrecht. Rechtsvergleich, völker- und europarechtliche Vorgaben und Perspektiven für das deutsche Recht* (2001).

ERIKSEN (2001)

E.O. Eriksen, 'Democratic or technocratic governance?' Paper is part of contributions to the Jean Monnet Working Paper No.6/01; *Mountain or Molehill?; A Critical Appraisal of the Commission White Paper on Governance.*

ERMACORA (1988)
F. Ermacora, *Grundriß der Menschenrechte in Österreich* (Vienna 1988).

ESTY (1994)
D. Esty, *Greening the GATT: Trade, Environment and the Future* (Washington DC 1994).

FRANCIONI (2001)
F. Francioni (ed.), *Environment, Human Rights and International Trade* (Oxford 2001).

GAJA (1999)
G. Gaja, *Introduzione al diritto comunitario* (Bari 1999).

HATJE (1998)
A. Hatje, *Die gemeinschaftsrechtliche Steuerung der Wirtschaftsverwaltung* (1998).

JANS (2000)
J.H. Jans, *European Environmental Law* (Groningen 2000).

JANS & VON DER HEIDE (2003)
J. H. Jans, A.-K. von der Heide, *Europäisches Umweltrecht* (Groningen 2003).

KAHL (1993)
Wolfgang Kahl, *Umweltprinzip und Gemeinschaftsrecht* (Heidelberg 1993).

O'KEEFFE (2000)
D. O'Keeffe, 'Exclusive, Concurrent and Shared Competence', in A. Dashwood & C. Hillion, *The General Law of EC External Relations* (London 2000), 179 *et seq.*

KISS AND SHELTON (1993)
A. Kiss and D. Shelton, *Manual of European Environmental Law* (Cambridge 1993).

KOSKENNIEMI (1998)
M. Koskenniemi, *International Law Aspects of the European Union* (The Hague 1998).

KRÄMER (1990)

L. Krämer, Zur innerstaatlichen Wirkung von Umwelt-Richtlinien der EWG, (1990) *WiVerw*, 138 *et seq.*

KRÄMER (1993)

L. Krämer, *European Environmental Law Casebook* (London 1993).

KRÄMER (2002)

L. Krämer, *Casebook on EU Environmental Law* (Oxford 2002).

KRÄMER (2002A)

L. Krämer, 'Die Rechtsprechung der EG-Gerichte zum Umweltschutz 2000 und 2001', (2002) *EuGRZ*, 483 *et seq.*

KRÄMER (2002B)

L. Krämer, *Europäisches Umweltrecht in der Rechtsprechung des EuGH* (Wien 2002).

KRÄMER (2003)

L. Krämer, 'Vertraulichkeit und Öffentlichkeit; Europäisches Vorverfahren und Zugang zu Informationen', in L. Krämer (editor), *Recht und Um-Welt; Essays in Honour of Prof. Dr. Gerd Winter* (Groningen 2003), 153-170.

KLEY-STRULLER (1995)

A. Kley-Struller, 'Schutz der Umwelt durch die EMRK' (1995) *EuGRZ* 507 *et seq.*

LOIBL (2002)

G. Loibl, 'The Role of the European Union in the Formation of International Environmental Law', in (2002) *YEEL*, 223 *et seq.*

MACLEOD (1996)

I. MacLeod, I. Hendry & S.Hyett, *The External Relations of the European Communities: A Manual of Law and Practice* (Oxford 1996).

MACRORY (2001)

R. Macrory, *Environmental integration and the European Charter of Fundamental Rights.* Paper presented to the Avosetta Group, Jan. 12/13, 2001. At: www.avosetta.org.

MCGOLDRICK (1997)

D. McGoldrick, *International Relations Law of the European Union* (London 1997).

MONTINI (2001)

M. Montini, 'The Necessity Principle as an Instrument to Balance Trade and the Protection of the Environment', in F. Francioni (ed.), *Environment, Human Rights and International Trade* (Oxford 2001), 135 *et seq.*

PERNICE (2000)

I. Pernice, Kompetenzabgrenzung im europäischen Verfassungsverbund, (2000) *JZ*, 866 *et seq.*

PETERSMANN (1995)

E.U. Petersmann, *International and European Law after the Uruguay Round* (London 1995).

REHBINDER (2000)

E. Rehbinder, 'Nachhaltigkeit als Prinzip des Umweltrechts: konzeptionelle Fragen', in: H.-P. Dolde (Hrsg.) *Umwelt im Wandel* (Berlin 2000).

ROSAS (2000)

A. Rosas, 'The European Union and Mixed Agreements', in A. Dashwood & C. Hillion, *The General Law of EC External Relations* (London 2000), 200 *et seq.*

SZCZEKALLA (2003)

P. Szczekalla, 'Allgemeine Rechtsgrundsätze', in Rengeling (ed.) *Handbuch zum europäischen und deutschen Umweltrecht (EUDUR)*, Volume I (Köln 2003).

STREINZ (1999)

R. Streinz, *Europarecht* (Würzburg 1999).

TEMMINK (2000)

H. Temmink, 'From Danish bottles to Danish bees: the dynamics of free movement of goods and environmental protection - a case law analysis' (2000) *Yearbook of European Environmental Law* Vol. 1, 61-102.

THIEME (2001)

D. Thieme, 'European Community External Relations in the Field of the Environment', in (2001) *EELR* 252 *et seq.*

VEDDER (2002)

H.H.B. Vedder, *Competion Law, Environmental Policy and Producer Responsibility* (Groningen 2002).

VERSCHUUREN (2003)

J. Verschuuren, *Principles of environmental law. The ideal of sustainable development and the role of principles of international, European and national environmental law* (Baden-Baden 2003).

WEGENER (1998)

B. Wegener, *Rechte des Einzelnen* (Baden-Baden 1998).

WIERS (2002)

J. Wiers, *Trade and Environment in the EC and the WTO* (Groningen 2002).

WINTER (1997)

G. Winter, *Alternativenprüfung im Prozess administrativer Entscheidungsbildung. Zugleich ein Beitrag zu einer Grundpflicht ökologischer Verhältnismäßigkeit* (Düsseldorf 1997).

WINTER (2000)

G. Winter, 'Die Steuerung grenzüberschreitender Abfallströme', in (2000) *Deutsches Verwaltungsblatt*, 657 *et seq.*

DE WITTE (2001)

Bruno De Witte, 'The Legal Status of the Charter: Vital Question or Non-issue?' (2001) *Maastricht Journal of European and Comparative Law*, 81-89.

Contributors

Gyula Bándi

Gyula Bándi (C.Sc., Dr. habil.) is professor of law and head of
the Environmental Law Chair of the Pázmány Péter Catholic University (Buda-
pest, Hungary). He teaches environmental and administrative law at other universities also, for example, the Eötvös Loránd University. He is coordinating the
post-graduate course in environmental law at the Eötvös Loránd University. He
is author of several books and articles, and editor of the *Environmental Pocket-
books* series. Gyula Bándi is member of the editorial board of the *Environmental
Encyclopedia*, the *European Law Review* and chairman of the editorial board of
the Hungarian *Environmental Protection Review*. He is founder and president
of the Environmental Management and Law Association, is practicing environmental law as an attorney and participates in different projects concerning
environmental law approximation in Hungary and SEE countries.

Astrid Epiney

Professor Astrid Epiney teaches law at the University of Fribourg (Switzerland). She graduated from the Johannes-Gutenberg-Universität
in Mainz (Germany) in 1989. After obtaining her Ph.D. in Mainz she took
her masters in law in Florence (Italy) in 1992. For the following two years she
worked as a researcher at the Institut de Hautes Etudes en Administration Pub-
lique (IDHEAP) in Lausanne (Switzerland) where she completed her *Habilita-
tion*. She was awarded the *venia legendi* for public law, international law and EC
law by the University of Mainz (Germany) in 1994. Since then she has been
teaching both the LL.B and LL.M degrees at the University of Fribourg along
with publishing a large number of articles and books.

Florian Ermacora

Dr. Florian Ermacora (1969) studied law at the Universities of
Innsbruck, Vienna and Paris (Paris-Assas). His doctoral thesis concerned the
distinction between waste and products under European and Austrian Law.
Between 1996 and 2000 Dr. Ermacora worked as an official of the EC Commission in the Waste Management Unit of DG Environment. His main responsibilities included general legal questions in relation to the application of EC waste
management law and the preparation of the Commission Proposal on Waste
Electrical and Electronic Equipment. Since January 2001 Dr. Ermacora has been
working for the Austrian Law Firm Schönherr Rechtsanwälte OEG in Vienna, in
particular in the areas of Energy Law, Environmental Law and general EC Law.
Dr. Ermacora has published various articles and books on EC environmental
and energy law and lectures regularly at conferences on EC Environmental and
Energy Law.

Jan H.Jans

is Professor of the Law of the European Union at the Europa Instituut, University of Amsterdam. He is a member of the Dutch Commission on Environmental Impact Assessment, Vice-Chairman of the Appeal Committee of the Netherlands Competition Authority and honorary judge at the District Court of Assen. He is also a member of the editorial boards of the *Journal of Environmental Law, SEW, Legal Issues of Economic Integration* and *The Columbian Journal of European Law.* He has published on Public Law, Constitutional Law, Environmental Law, European Law, European Public Law and European Environmental Law. His book *European Environmental Law* (second edition Europa Law Publishing) is generally regarded as one of the leading publications on European environmental law.

Ludwig Krämer

Ludwig Krämer is a judge at the Landgericht Kiel. He is at leave with the Commission of the European Community where he is in charge of an administrative unit 'environmental governance' in the Directorate General for the Environment. He is Honorary Professor at Bremen University, Visiting Professor at the University College London and lectures on European and international environmental law at the College of Europe in Bruges (Belgium). He has published books and articles on European environmental law.

Massimiliano Montini

Massimiliano Montini holds a law degree (J.D.) from the University of Siena (1994) and an LL.M. in European Law from University College London (1996). He is currently a Lecturer at the University of Siena in the fields of International Law and European Union Law. He has considerable research experience especially in the field of International and EC Environmental law. He is the co-ordinator of a post-graduate course in environmental law annually organised by the University of Siena. Moreover, he is a fully qualified practising lawyer, a member of the Italian Bar, and he provides consultancy services in particular on environmental matters.

Gerd Winter

Gerd Winter studied law and sociology in Würzburg, Freiburg/ Br., Lausanne, Göttingen and Konstanz. Since 1973 he has been Professor of Public Law, European Law and Sociology of Law at the University of Bremen. He has been Director of the Research Centre for European Environmental Law at that university since 1995. From 1992 – 1997 he was a member of the Independent Expert Commission for the Codification of German Environmental Law and since 1999 a member of National Committee on Global Environmental Change

Research. He is also a member of the IUCN Law Commission. On a regular basis he has acted as legal consultant in administrative and environmental law for, among others, the Russian Federation, Georgia and Tajikistan and, in Germany, as counsel in major environmental law cases. Gerd Winter has published on administrative law, environmental law, EU law and the sociology of law. One of his recent publications concerns the reform of the European chemicals regulation.